POINTING
THE WAY

POINTING
THE WAY

Spiritual Insights
from the
SFAS EMES

Rabbi
Yehudah Aryeh Leib Alter

translated by
MOSHE A. BRAUN

JASON ARONSON INC.
Northvale, New Jersey
London

This book was set in 12 pt. Berkeley by Alpha Graphics of Pittsfield, New Hampshire, and printed and bound by Book-mart Press of North Bergen, New Jersey.

10 9 8 7 6 5 4 3 2 1

Library of Congress Cataloging-in-Publication Data

Braun, Moshe A.
    Pointing the way: spiritual insights from the Sfas Emes Rabbi Yehudah Aryeh Leib Alter / Moshe A. Braun.
        p.   cm.
    ISBN 1-56821-996-2 (alk. paper)
    1. Hasidism.   2. Judaism—Doctrines.   3. Alter, Judah Aryeh Leib, 1874–1905—Teachings.   I. Title.
BM198.2.B76   1997
296.3—dc20   96–27842
                                                                CIP

Manufactured in the United States of America. Jason Aronson Inc. offers books and cassettes. For information and catalog write to Jason Aronson Inc., 230 Livingston Street, Northvale, New Jersey 07647.

לזכר נשמת

מוה"ר ישראל בן הגאון וצדיק תמים
מוה"ר חיים ברוין ז"ל
מעיר באניהאד שם אמו אסתר שינדל

מרת מלכה בת איש החסד
מוה"ר משה אשר זילבער ז"ל
מעיר סאבאסלא שם אמה גיטל

מוה"ר משה מרדכי בן התמים
מוה"ר שמואל זאב הי"ד
מעיר סאלאש שם אמו יוטא

מרת מלכה בת הרה"ח
מוה"ר יצחק אייזיק הי"ד
מעיר סעמיהאלי שם אמה לאה

Contents

Acknowledgments

I would like to thank Arthur Kurzweil of Jason Aronson Inc., and his staff, for doing such a great job with this book and my previous work, *The Jewish Holy Days*.

I would also like to thank my wife Leah for her many years of admonishing me to persevere. May this book point the way for our children: Zevy, Pessie, and Chevele; Shaindy, Sruly, Surala, Shmuel Zevy, and Gitty; Mutty, Gitty, Yisroel Reuven, and Chayala; Chavy, Daniel, Yisroel, and Yehudah; Chaya, Yitty, and Yosef Yitzchok. May we always meet along the way to share joy and good tidings.

Introduction

One of the hallmarks of the Hasidic movement was the type of lecture the rebbe offered his Hasidim. Departing from the style of the formal and often eloquent rabbinical sermons of the day, which combined scholarship with oratory, the Hasidic lecture sought intimacy with the listener. Using a short anecdote or Biblical interpretation, the rebbe would imbue his listeners with awe of God and an urgency to serve Him with every sinew.

This inspiration was first received by small knots of Hasidim, who in turn passed it on to an ever-larger circle of the community. The teachings conveyed a mystical joy in the communion of God and man, and provided a cheerful affirmation of life, with an emphasis on empathy, humanity, and love. They counselled against abstinence and self-affliction, encouraging their audience instead to hallow all passion and delight in the service of God, to accept life with enthusiasm, gratitude, and perseverance, to pursue kindness and mercy, and to live with an inward faith far above ceremonial piety. They praised the virtue of charity, the folly of human possessions, and the importance of spiritual values; they re-established the link of the individual with the community, the people of Israel, and humanity as a whole; and they demanded worship with sincerity and fervor, and stressed compassion even for the sinner.

The goal of the Hasidic discourse is to set the heart and mind, the passions and reasoning of the Hasid aright, focused on the path of God. We can compare this, said a sage, to a man lost completely in a forest. Suddenly, a bolt of lightning flashed and the entire forest was lit up like day. Every tree, flower, and blade of grass was clearly visible, and for that instant the one who was lost saw unflinchingly and precisely where he was.

That bolt of lightning is the rebbe's discourse. And with it, the soul of the listener is lit up; its light shining into every nook and cranny of his heart and mind. He sees with cosmic clarity where he is and where he is headed.

The discourse raises our spiritual consciousness, which precedes even wisdom, as it is written, "The beginning of wisdom is the fear of God." (Ps. 111:10) This fear of God is the awareness of God's presence without which there is no wisdom. It also gives us tools for introspection; tools which can make one's work more precise. It helps us mend the torn, repair the broken, and straighten the crooked, as it is written, "Let us search and examine our ways, and return to God." (Lam. 3:40)

"Torah," means to teach and show the way, and those who study its holy books are aware of its awesome breadth. As Job said, "Its measure is longer than the earth and deeper than the sea." (Job 11:9) It is a cram-packed storage house of knowledge, from the practical laws of commerce, to the esoteric solutions of cosmic mysteries and the purpose of Being. It is the towering treasure, both for the whole of the Jewish nation, as well as for each individual. It is also the greatest gift to mankind, as it is written ". . .that will be proof of your wisdom and discernment to other peoples . . . " (Deut. 4:6)

Just as a prized possession is often studied and admired by its owner, so too is the Torah. Each one must study it more and more often and find in it new wisdom and guidance.

No doubt anyone possessing wisdom wants to grow spiritually, in awareness, and in good deeds. And there is no better way to grow than by studying, delving into, and meditating on Torah wisdom. Therefore, I have gathered and made available to the reader a wealth of spiritual guidance taught by the great Hasidic master and teacher, the author of the Sefas Emes, Rabbi Yehudah Aryeh Leib Alter, the second leader of the Hasidic dynasty of Gur.

Born to the first Gerer Rebbe, Rabbi Mordechai Alter (who was the only son of the Chidushei Ha'rim) in Warsaw on the eve of rosh chodesh Iyar in 1847, he was orphaned as a young boy and educated by his grandfather, one of the greatest Torah sages of that time. Even at a young age, he learned Torah with great diligence, eighteen hours a day. To visiting scholars his grandfather would say, "Look at my grandson how he studies Torah!" When the grandfather passed away, the Hasidim wanted to appoint him as the next Gerer Rebbe. Being merely nineteen years old, he refused, and instead went as a pupil to the Rebbe of Aleksander. Four years later the Rebbe of Aleksander passed away and again the Hasidim urged him to take on the yoke of leadership. This time he accepted. He molded Gur as a center of

Hasidut, attracting tens of thousands of followers from all over Europe. His commentaries on the Talmud made him renowned as a great Torah scholar as well as a brilliant leader. For more than thirty years he counseled his followers to live with fervent devotion to the Torah, both in study and deed. In 1905, at the age of fifty-seven, a few days before he passed away, he set down the last of his written words, "Lips of truth, S'fas Emes, stand firm forever" (Prov. 12:19). Because these were the last words of his earthly sojourn, his sons chose them as a lasting tribute and collectively named his writings S'fas Emes.

These are the seminal ideas culled from his weekly discourses which his thousands of Hasidim came to hear every Sabbath at Tish, the rebbe's table. The rebbe used Torah passages of the weekly portion to weave these ideas into a fabric of Hasidic teachings. While they are appealing within the context of the Torah verses, they have a special beauty standing independently. Essentially bare, they speak succinctly and directly to the soul of man. They instruct and enlighten, rebuke and demand, uplift and inspire: in a word, they *point the way*.

Moshe Braun
Teves, 5755

1

Hidden or Revealed

Mixture of Good and Evil

Don't think that because you want to be good and do the right thing, that it will be easy. On the contrary, you should expect to have difficulties, because the world is all mixed up. It is all a mixture of good and evil, and difficult to separate. But God, with great mercy, gave us the Torah to sift the good from the evil. The Torah contains, in coded form perhaps, the perfect world of goodness, which God used as plans for the creation. It is up to each of us to study the Torah, or at least adhere to its commandments. And when we do, the Torah's light, which is hidden in nature, becomes revealed. That light within helps us discern the good, and we are able to do right.

God's Providence Is Hidden

We know that God gives us everything. So why don't we even notice? Days pass, and we act as if we don't know that it was God who took care of us. This is only because God's kingdom is concealed; His caring for His creatures is not evident or obvious. This is alluded to in the holy tongue: The Hebrew for "world" is *olam*, almost sounding like the word *heh-lom*, "hidden." We have to work hard to find the hidden part of the world, God's providence. Abraham, the first *Ivri*, worked very hard, by searching and investigating. Finally, he discovered the Master of the world, who tends to every detail. We too, must search and find the Master. And when we do, we must thank Him for His kindness always and every instant.

Finding the Good

The world is a mixture of good and evil, not easily separated. Should one ever hope to find the good, it will be with much effort. That work is called *derech eretz*, and it precedes Torah. Torah separates the good from the evil, while *derech eretz* is the work to make the result possible.

Heaven on Earth

The heavens seem remote from our earthly life. Yet both the physical and the spiritual world are one and the same. Why then do they seem so different? Because the physical world is a confusion of good and evil, while the spiritual one is of clearly identified parts.

We ought to approach our life with respect and reverence. Even if it seems lowly, nevertheless the earth is a heavenly place. And though we experience instances of depravity, those are merely bits of evil mingled with the spiritual goodness. We should always strive to separate and see the good and holy in all things and live a hallowed life.

Hide, Seek, and Find

The Creator is hidden in nature, and we wonder why. Why couldn't the honor of God be easily found? Why do we have to search for Him?

The truth is that God is so far removed from the physical world that there is really no way to comprehend Him. We literally do not have the means to understand His being. Our eyes cannot see Him, our ears cannot hear Him, nor can we sense Him in any other way. We only recognize Him through His deeds. Therefore, it is only because of His hiddenness, that we can find Him.

Let us therefore take courage when we do not find God, when we don't experience His power and strength. That is precisely when we will find Him.

Behind Darkness the Brightest Light

The physical crust of the world covers the inner spiritual spark in each created thing. The milder the spirituality, the less it is blocked by the outer crust. And the more intense and holier the spirituality, the more it is blocked. This is like someone wearing sunglasses in very dim light. The shaded glasses hardly block a barely shining light. But when there is a brilliant light, the shaded glasses block it extremely.

When we encounter spiritual darkness, and all seems hidden and hopeless, then we can expect to find great spiritual light.

Secrets

Some spiritual sparks hidden in the physical world can be found by *tzaddikim*, "righteous people," who seek them. And even if the *tzaddik* does not know where the secret is, still he leaves no effort untried until he finds it.

The Soul in the Body

The material nature of the body covers the spiritual light of the soul. When the opacity of the body is removed, the light of the soul is revealed.

To Be Part of the Whole

The kingdom of God is concealed within the natural world. Although few look for it, and even fewer work for its revelation, the creation as a whole desires revelation always. Therefore any creature who negates his being to the collective Will becomes part of that desire. Especially when we observe God's commandments, we negate our being to *Klal Yisroel*, "the collective of the Jewish people," and are able to do each mitzvah properly.

Light in the Darkness

Every bit of spiritual light that enters this world is accompanied by a corresponding darkness. It is clothed in the darkness, and man's task is to set it free, release it, and make it manifest.

Higher than Angels

Every created thing has a spiritual spark which is its vitality. However, that inner core is hidden and is not recognized by most. The Jewish people, by ignoring the outer crust, realize and witness that God created the universe and that His will keeps it alive.

In this activity, the Jewish people are on a higher level than the angels. Angels call to each other and ask, "Where is the place of His honor?" and respond, "Blessed is the honor of God from its place." They are witnesses to the omnipresence of God.

But without the Jewish people God's kingdom would never be recognized, neither today nor in the past. And since His kingdom "needs" the Jewish people, they can ask God for special favors. But they do not. They merely do their "job." They repeatedly tell mankind to ignore the outer crust, the laws of nature. Instead, to heed the spiritual spark, God's energy in all things. And they do it purely for God's sake, so that God's plan may be fulfilled. Thus they are higher than the angels.

God's Hiding Places

The world has many hiding places. They are places of darkness where the presence of God is obscure and concealed. Both the righteous and the wicked walk in those places. The wicked, not seeing God there, decide that it is a good place for their evil deeds. They will do their wickedness, and need not worry about punishment.

The righteous walk through those very places. But they go there to reveal the kingdom of God, and show that there is no place where He is not found.

God mocks the wicked, "You try to hide from me in the very hiding places which I have created?" And to the righteous He says, "Be assured that I am with you wherever you go, even in the darkest places." The wicked are exposed for their evil, and the righteous are rewarded by having their good deeds become known.

A king, for security reasons, built underground hiding places for his army. One day, rebels attacked the palace. When the king gave chase, the rebels hid in the king's secret tunnels. The king followed them, and yelled, "So, you want to hide in the very hiding places which I have built!"

Secrets Are Revealed

Although God's kingdom is concealed, the righteous are sensitive and find it in the most obscure places. They are blessed with the ability to feel the spiritual in places and situations. After searching, the secret is revealed to them.

Two Levels of the Spirit

There are the lower levels of the spirit, and the higher levels. The lower levels are occasionally concealed in the envelope of the material world. Even the higher spirit, although high and lofty and easily revealed, is nevertheless concealed because of its lofty nature. That portion of the soul is only manifest on special occasions.

The Will of God Revealed

"And I pray to You, God, in an opportune time . . ." (Psalms 69:14).

There really is no fluctuation in the will and desire of God concerning the creation. There are, however, times in which the will of God is concealed, and times in which the will of God is clearly revealed. This is especially true on the day of *Shabbos*, the day in which God had the most satisfaction from His creation. Similarly, there are also moments for each individual in which God's desire for the world is revealed, and that is the occasion for his prayer.

Turning Away

Nature is a world of good and evil in a mixture. Man lives in that world, and therefore has a hard time discerning between the two. He is plagued by this problem his entire life. What can he do? He must turn away from completely physical pursuits and put their attractions to rest. Then he can focus on his inner being, spirit, and gain a deep understanding of the divine path.

The Spark Is Revealed

It is a divine spark which gives life to every living thing, but it is concealed. *Sohd*, the Hebrew word for "secret," has a numerical value of seventy, the number of Israelite souls which descended into Egypt. The Jewish people, the divine spark of the nations, was hidden among them. And that secret is revealed to the degree that the creature is a vessel for God's kingdom. When one acts and lives with God's principles, one then brings to light His kingdom.

Hiding the Good

During all of man's life he strives to rise higher and higher spiritually. For each step he takes upward, evil struggles against him even harder. The more difficult it becomes to rise to the next step, the more and more potent becomes the effort of the righteous. This cycle is repeated over and over in each of our lifetimes.

What is really happening? Each spiritual level that is attained is soon hidden by evil. The fuss and fight that evil puts up conceals that level from man's eyes. But the concealment makes possible the attainment of a level even higher than the current one. Therefore, whenever we see that good is hidden we can be sure that it is to enable us to strive to a higher spiritual path.

Hidden Treasure

In the realm of commerce, if one accumulates money without much effort he owns it just as if he had struggled for it. In the spiritual realm, however, the good achieved with ease is not nearly as good as that achieved with struggle. There are spiritual treasures buried deep within; the only way to get to them is by hard work and struggle.

Time of Yearning

Ever since the creation there has been a mixture of good and evil in all aspects of the world. This includes a person's potential, talents, and abilities. If one is not aware of his own abilities, he at least does not suffer. But if he should discover a special talent, such as singing, and is then prevented from expressing it, he will be in pain. We have to realize, though, that every virtue has its manifest and its concealed side. Love, the expression of caring for another, has its concealed side in bad love, as lust, incest, and love for the forbidden. The arousal of feeling for another comes from the virtue of love, God's love for the world. But the concealed other side is forbidden love.

Each spiritual level's attainment is accompanied by opposition and hiddenness, and then hunger to live on the new level. Hunger is pain. But a servant of God will understand that the pain is a yearning to be there. He is there and he will prevail. He will come out of concealment.

The deepest spiritual truth is that in the hunger, in the concealment, on the wrong side, on the other side, the spiritual light is present, but hidden. If one recognizes this, one will not be annoyed in times of hiddenness.

Descent into Darkness

There are three levels descending lower and lower in level of holiness. First there is the root of God's gifts. That is pure light. Then as it descends and enters this world, it becomes a balanced mixture of light and darkness. Finally, at the earthly level, darkness covers the light completely.

Keeping Secrets

The spirit of God is both hidden and revealed. On one hand it is hidden, and its infinite, powerful light is protected within the corpus of the Jewish nation. On the other hand, that body reveals God's kingdom, and points to the spirit of God in all things. Yet, the glow remains hidden within it.

The nations of the world, from afar, sense the great light coming forth from Zion, from the nation of Israel, and want to come close to it. And when they do they can't find the light, and wonder where it is.

Similarly there is silence and speaking. The one who can keep silent and protect his speech within, can also speak.

Harsh Words

God created the world with ten commands, very soft and quiet words, which were then hidden within nature. It took the ten plagues, emphatic and harsh words, to uncover them, by demonstrating that God is the ruler over all.

The Body Blocks the Light

Our souls are glowing lights which cannot be seen through the opacity of our material bodies. The less we emphasize and give dominion to the body, the more translucent it becomes, allowing the soul's light to shine through.

Our deeds are witnesses for the Creator. And we need to make a clear statement, without mixing in purely materialistic interests. Then the kingdom of God is declared and the light shines to all creatures.

The Answer Is Already There

When our prayers are answered we feel as if we caused the solution, the recovery, or the redemption. In the spiritual realm it is the opposite. God had already prepared the solution, and we are only worthy to receive it because of our prayers and repentance.

Open, Closed

God is the one and only. His being is entirely different than anything found in the material world. Therefore He is neither totally revealed nor concealed. We experience Him as being constantly revealed and concealed in a cycle. The same is true of the Jewish nation as a whole and of each individual member. They are likened to the rose which is open during the day and closed at night. Their greatness is never fully seen by the world, but is in the depths of their being.

The secret of life lies in the revelation and hiding of the light. As the light is hidden, so is its revelation imminent. And as it is revealed, so is its concealment imminent. We see this in the body, with the opening and closing of valves, and in the work of the immune system. The entire life flows through man's veins displaying concealment and revelation as the light of glowing embers lights and dims and lights again.

2

Source of Life

In God's Hand

God puts life into you every instant. No matter how intelligent, talented, and independent you may be, it is He who keeps you alive. You are as an "ax in the hands of the woodsman," totally in God's control. Whether you obey God or transgress His will with sin and abomination, still your breath of life is from Him.

Only with Kindness

God would have created the world with strict judgment, but He foresaw that thus it couldn't last. He therefore created it with loving-kindness also. Similarly, we too must always plan to do everything with strict judgment, with utmost care

13

and precision. Before we do a mitzvah, we must learn how to perform it to its minutest detail. And although we cannot finish our deed with perfection, the mercy of God will accompany us to its completion.

Although we may plan, we can never finish anything without the help of God. But don't expect to be helped unless you put your entire energy into the planning. If you do, you will be amazed at the ease with which you complete it.

Whose Achievement?

When one is sent to complete a mission and does, he returns to the one who sent him. "I have just returned from the mission, and wish to report that it has been completed," he reports, thus giving the credit of the results to the one who sent him. Otherwise, the messenger may believe that all the credit belongs to him.

Similarly, man is sent to earth with a mission. Its plan and its lifelong assignment is all in the Torah. Each time he is successful and completes a task, such as a mitzvah or good deed, he must return it to God who sent him, and report, "God, I have completed one task. What do I do next?" He thus pleads with God for energy to continue. He will get his wish, too, but only in the measure of the enthusiasm with which he returned his previous mitzvah to God.

The New World

The world, although monotonously old, is really always fresh and new. Were it not always new, it would long ago have perished and faded into oblivion.

The simplest example of this can be found among the animals. Those animals that were not able to regenerate and renew their species became extinct and are no more. The world's renewal, however, is deeper than that. God created and constantly re-creates the world. He must desire the world with His purely free will every instant. For had He not desired it at any time, the entire universe would cease to be. It would return to nothingness. Thus there is a new desire from God every instant, and that desire causes the world to be created again and again.

But all this is hidden. To all appearances the world just exists without any outside intervention, as some wise men in every generation have mistakenly thought. It is the Torah that reveals that the world is constantly new. Its message is clear from the very beginning, ". . . God created the heaven and the earth . . ."

Suppose then, that upon arising, we look at the world before we begin our daily grind. Which world will we work in? The old monotonous one that has been around for thousands of years, or the brand-new one which God just now created? And for whom? It was created for man. But how could man ever be aware of this truth? Only through the teachings of the Torah.

Therefore each day, before we do anything, the very first thing upon arising must be Torah study. With it we get a fresh look at the world, and realize our awesome responsibility. What will we do in this world which has just been created?

The Home of Mankind

When creatures are in their natural environment, they are at rest and peaceful. Removed from their natural homes, they are restless. Every creature has a place and a home.

There it is able to live and thrive. But remove it, separate it from its sustenance and life, and it has problems.

The place of every creature is to stand before God in total submission. That is its true nature: totally dependent on God for its very life. Those who think they are independent of God are mistaken, and out of their natural home. However, one can easily be misled when one observes the accomplishments that man does "on his own." One can easily mistake that for independence from God.

What can help man realize the truth about his home? Only the Torah. It is the doorway to the home of every member of mankind. The home of all creatures is the fear and awe of God. And those who have it are at home and thriving.

Stealing from God?

Why does one steal? Because he momentarily denies that God, as master, gives to those He wants and takes from others. Whatever you are supposed to get will come your way, and you needn't take it from another.

Similarly, we must acknowledge that the very life of every created being is given to him by God only. If we use a thing against God's will, we are as mistaken as a thief. Therefore we mustn't waste any of the energy which God gives so generously. By realizing that God's honor fills the world, we will increasingly respect Him and follow His commandments.

Help of God

We always need God's help and support. It is impossible for any creature to live even for a second without God. But those who have complete faith and trust don't experience weakness when their help comes. The others, whose faith is weaker, feel their weakness and ineptitude as they are being helped. Regardless if one experiences his strength as coming from within or without, one cannot survive without it.

The Natural World Needs Help

A person is physical, fallible, limited, and impermanent. He is a creature and is in critical need of help. And even the righteous *tzaddikim*, who constantly aspire to do God's will, need to be helped. They cannot possibly fulfill their noble desire without His support.

This is because a creature is limited and is by definition in need. As long as one is true to one's nature, one will be in need of help.

Our ancestor Abraham set us on a different course. He broke away from the natural world of cause and effect. He risked his life, negated his entire being, to do God's will. Therefore he rose to a realm outside of nature. Similarly, a *tzaddik* with total resignation does not need the kind of help required by other creatures.

God Rules over Them All

In the world of nature there is a hierarchical relationship among the creatures. There are lowly creatures which become the food for higher-level creatures, as in food chains: thus lettuce is the food for the slug, who is eaten by the ground beetle, who in turn is eaten by the shrew, who finally finds his end in the barn owl. This hierarchy is alluded to in the Haggadah's fable of the one sheep eaten by the cat, who is eaten by the dog, who is beaten by a stick, which is burned by the fire, then extinguished by water, that is licked up by a cow, who is slaughtered by the *shochet*, himself taken by the Angel of Death, and who is finally liquidated by the Creator Himself. Similarly, we have the king and his servants, the master and his apprentice. And even in the spiritual sphere, there are the *serafim*, *ofanim*, and angels of a variety of levels, one over the other, higher and higher up to the throne of God.

The apparent conclusion we can draw from this is that in the world of nature some are masters and some are slaves. Or as others express this, some have power while others are powerless. The truth, according to our faith, is that, appearances aside, God is the total and absolute ruler and master over all creatures. From the loftiest celestial spirit to the lowliest creature, God rules over them all. Therefore, although it may appear as if the ground beetle rules over the slug, the dog rules over the cat, the king rules over his servant, the nations over the Jewish people, it is all an illusion. God rules over each and every one of them. God rules over the Jewish people, and on occasion puts them in the hands of other nations. But He, and He alone, is their king, master, and ruler. And he who understands this axiom of faith is immediately free. He is transported from the illusions of the natural world to the world of eternal truth, where all creatures are in awe of their creator who sustains them every instant.

God, the Source of Energy

Analyzing the world truthfully, we conclude that the creation draws its energy from a single source. Searching for the source of energy in coal, we discover elements and chemical changes, atomic particles, and finally energy. When we analyze the source of energy in man, we again find chemical exchanges, atomic particles, and finally energy. And the source of the energy in all things is the Creator, the one and only master of the world.

Thus, in seeking the truth, and being truthful in our quest, we must admit that our search eventually leads us to the Creator. And if we have not yet come to that conclusion, it is because we have not yet searched enough.

Only to Hear the Word of God

The ears of the Jewish people are tuned-in to the voice of God. They strain to hear any message addressed to them. Their very being awakes to the spiritual. They negate all messages from elsewhere—even their desires, hopes, and cravings—and listen only for God's message. Their desire to know is not for their ego; their quest is merely for knowledge of God.

Others may desire to know because of pride in "their" knowledge. They want to perfect "their" deeds; although noble, their efforts are merely for themselves. The nations may even humble themselves to God, because they know that it is the path to understanding, as an apprentice humbles himself to his master for the favor of teachings. The Jewish people, on the other hand, want to know more and more about God so they can relate to Him with proper humility.

Let us therefore be uplifted by and be sensitive to the word of God, and not allow our deeds to distract us.

Master of All Events

The most fundamental belief is that God created the universe. In addition to that, He is the ruler Who controls every single thing, by giving it life and making it happen. The first we must believe; once we do, we realize, with an obvious clarity, that He is the one Who controls the world.

God Protects Us

God promised the Jewish people that those who curse them will themselves be cursed. This teaches us that no matter what country we find ourselves in, He is ready to protect our integrity as a people and guarantee our survival.

Independence

Capitalism thrives on independence. In America and throughout the world the theme of independence has great importance. And as noble an aspiration as it may be, it is a false basis for a relationship with God. God is the source of life for all creatures, and to be independent of Him is certain death. If we want life we must be a vessel for its source. God has a plan for the world, and either we resign ourselves to it or we don't. Those who do are true to their beings and live a life of truth; those who refuse live falsely and without fulfillment.

Without God, Nothing

Every creature, including man, must know that he is nothing more than a creature. To the degree that he recognizes this fact, he is able to bring offspring into the world. When man recognizes that God does everything with His free will, his deeds merge with the spiritual world and endure. But the deeds of one who thinks that he is independent of the Creator are merely physical and impermanent.

We need to carefully adjust our thoughts prior to our deeds, to stand before God as creatures empty of all content, waiting to be filled with life by our Creator.

Only with God

In a spiritual high, one might boast to oneself about one's "own" great accomplishment and forget God. Therefore, we must always remember our slavery and liberation from Egypt. Without God, no spiritual accomplishment is possible— only oppression, misery, and torture. To be free, to develop and become somebody, we must have God.

Stamped as God's Servant

The act of circumcision is not performed merely to remove the foreskin, but expresses the willingness to be stamped and identified as a lifelong servant of God. Similarly, giving the tithe from one's field is not merely apportioning a small amount for the poor: rather, it is an acknowledgement that the entire field belongs to God and was granted as a gift to its owner. Therefore, these mitzvos are not merely small acts, but influence our entire life.

Until Birth

There are three realms: space, time, and spirit. The three are intertwined and related; what is true in one is also true in the other. The formation of a child takes place in the realm of spirit. First there is nothing, then the formation of the child begins. The vitality, which will be the child, is protected throughout the gestation period, until a mature baby is born. Similarly, in time and space, God watches the sacred kernel till it comes to fruition.

3

Improvement

Lifting the Lowly

Moving higher and higher spiritually is different from climbing a ladder. On a ladder we move from rung to rung, leaving the lower ones behind and climbing to the higher. Not so with spiritual steps. When we move up spiritually, our responsibility to lift those at lower levels increases. With each step we advance, we need to descend and lift up those at the level below and raise them to where we are. That is, after all, the reason why we are up there.

Similarly, the Jewish nation as a whole descends to the depths of the deeps in order to rise to the highest heights.

Yearning

God is perfect, while the world—man included—is full of imperfections. What is worse, our life is full of distractions, sapping our very energy. How can we ever hope to do the will of God? It is only because we yearn and hope to do what is right: we desire perfection although we know that it is unattainable. Therefore, God helps us in our quest to do His will.

Who Is Perfect?

God is perfect and whole. All creatures share an imperfection in that they are creatures. They are not God, and therefore are not perfect. Only those who cleave to God can share in His perfection. On the other hand, whoever thinks he is perfect is obviously mistaken. And what is the cause of his mistake? His total lack of perfection causes him to see perfection in himself. He doesn't realize that only God has it.

The degree of one's perfection depends on knowing how lacking one is. The ones who think that they are totally lacking may receive perfection from God. The ones who think they are perfect, and thereby totally cut off from God, have none.

Spiritual Symmetry

The deepest part of us is hidden until we have offspring. Then it is revealed. Similarly, our physical deeds are not merely what is seen. They are connected to the spiritual realm; whatever we do on earth is reflected in the heavenly sphere. Our good deeds reveal a deeper spiritual connection, and are therefore as offspring.

The Colors of God

God appears differently to each person. And if we could express this as seeing colors, then God appears as a different color to each one. As no two hearts are alike, neither is the color that is seen—the conception of God—the same in the hearts of any two people.

Honor Belongs to God Only

The Almighty, blessed be His name, deserves all the honor. No other creature deserves honor in the presence of God. When the king sits in the throne room and is being honored by visitors, it is wrong to give honor to anyone else. Therefore a creature, as we all are, ought to run from honor. It is not meant for him, but is the garment of the Creator. When we do all we can to avoid being honored, the honor reverts back to the Master of all honor. We honor God by avoiding receiving honor. Such a person, who increases the honor of God, God will honor, and therefore honor accrues to him.

Those who run after honor are chasing a commodity that does not belong to them, and they will not attain it. On the other hand, those who want all honor for the Creator will in the end be honored too, because they brought honor to Him.

Each Day a New Chance

The essence of every human being is his soul, which is whole and without blemish. He is sent to the physical realm to change his potential goodness into reality. And since his nature is physical, he is mortal and his time is limited. He must accomplish all his tasks within his lifespan, a definite and limited amount of time. Therefore, his striving for perfection is bounded by, and dependent on, time.

God renews the creation each and every day, and with each renewal a new chance is created for achieving perfec-

tion. Each day we get a new chance to negate the physical
world and make it a garment for the spiritual. We make each
day special, each day different, and each day worthwhile.

Of what use is each new day? Each new day brings new
understanding of God and His ways. Thus, each day is bound
to God and the spiritual realm, and is transformed into
spirituality.

According to the Effort

The honor of God's kingdom is hidden in the world. However, it is revealed to those who work to reveal it, according to the amount of effort that each puts into it.

To Reach Perfection

Each person has a name that expresses the task for which
he was created. If he works at his task all his life, he will get
closer and closer to completing it and reaching perfection.
But man is unable to complete his task because he is a physical being, and imperfect. Only in death, when he sheds his
physical shell, is he able to reach perfection.

Circumcision

In the mitzvah of circumcision we draw a holy spirit onto
the boy's body by changing nature: this will prevent him
from drowning in materialistic pursuits. Later he too will
draw holy souls from heaven and bring children into the
world. Similarly, those who work to change their habits
allow God's holiness to rest on them, and thus have the
power to beget others who will do the same.

Minding Whose Business?

Although in commerce everyone should mind their own business, it is not so in the realm of the spirit. Everyone needs to mind everyone's spiritual business: the tribe must survive and be perpetuated, and its way of life must not weaken nor be replaced by another. And God's promise to each member of the tribe is that He will be there to help him complete his spiritual undertaking. God will forsake no one, nor allow any soul to get lost forever. Each will be found and set straight.

Lost Opportunities

When the soul of man stands in judgment before the throne of God and face to face with the ultimate truth, it will have shame. Not only the wicked, but even the most righteous who strived his entire life to achieve holiness and spirituality will have shame. Because no matter how much he did, he allowed some emotion, some talent, some thought or speech to go to waste. And in the hour of truth he will see how much light was contained in that trifling moment, and he will be very pained that he allowed that opportunity to slip by. He will mourn not only for what evil he has done, but also for all the good that he could have done.

Limb by Limb

The very first "thought" of God before the creation was of the Jewish people. They are the purpose of the creation. And from the beginning to the end, the body of the Jewish people develops limb by limb till it is complete. Our forefathers

were the "head" of our people, and each generation is another limb which those holy brains are to direct. Thus they
progress till the holy intellect gets feet, too.

Remembering One's Name

Each star in heaven has a name and gives its own particular light. Similarly, each Jew is a star in God's spiritual
firmament with a name that defines the type of light he gives
to the world. It is most difficult to always remember one's
name, to not forget the particular mission one must perform; and it is a great accomplishment when one continues to light the darkness with his particular light.

God's Name

The truth of God's existence has no name: it is indescrib-
able and incomprehensible. On the other hand, God's deeds
have names: they are revealed and understood. Our task is
to connect our name to His name, our life to His life, our
meaning to His meaning.

Root of Wisdom

The physical world parallels the spiritual world. There are
therefore two causalities: spiritual roots beget physical results, and physical deeds alter spiritual realms. The root,
however, of all physical deeds is in the lofty heavenly realms
beyond human comprehension. From there it descends,
shell by thinnest shell, till it reaches the material world.
Although we may feel sure of ourselves, and without the
slightest doubt, results can be contrary: they were thus at

their roots and we couldn't possibly have known them. Spiritual roots are beyond human comprehension. Even godlike figures such as Moses, who could see through many layers of the spiritual world, could not see to the last of them.

Man has to submit himself to the root of all wisdom. He does this layer by layer. When he rises and matures spiritually, he realizes that what he thought was right was not so right. When he develops more, he again reevaluates his deeds and sees that the not so right was wrong, and the right was not so right.

This can go on and on, layer by infinitesimal layer. Finally he reaches a point beyond which he cannot go. All he can do then is to submit his entire being to the root of all. Thus he reaches the ultimate wisdom.

Divine Imagination

The universe would never survive the exactitude and severity of God's judgment. Although the laws of nature are "unerring and uniform," the dealings of men are not nearly perfect, but are full of lies, deceit, and wickedness. Therefore, the world needs great divine mercy in order to survive. There is a place, however, where even a human being can come close to the perfection intended for him: in his thoughts. Man can imagine the same perfect world that God imagines for mankind. The Torah is this very divine imagination in written form. Each of us can exert and struggle with his thoughts and keep them within the exactness of the divine imagination. Although we are imperfect, we must still maintain a mind dreaming of perfection, a spot in this imperfect universe where the judgment of God can give a verdict of innocence.

The Pain of the Soul

A Gentile asked Rabbi Eliazar, "You say that you are close to the King, so why are your people always in some pain or another, while the other nations live in tranquility?" Rabbi Eliazar answered, "We are like the heart, which feels every pain and worry, while the other nations are like the other parts of the body" (Zohar, Num. 28).

Similarly, the soul of man also would feel every nuance of spiritual pain. Unfortunately, we allow our material interests to dominate and desensitize us to things of the spirit. Therefore, we don't feel it.

The Summit Is Beyond Us

We work one step at a time to reach the highest level of holiness, and it seems as if the steps are leading there. Once we arrive there, however, we realize that the holiness has been there all the time. It was we who had to be raised to that level in order to be there.

Climbers were slowly ascending to the summit of a mountain. After an arduous climb, pitching tents, and backbreaking work, they reached the summit. Then they realized that the summit was there during their entire climb, only they had to reach it.

Honor of Kings

Kings need to be honored, but the honor of one king cancels the honor of another king: either this one gets honor, or the other one does. Not so with God's honor: the honor of all who seek honor comes from God's own honor. They all get honor, and His does not cancel theirs.

Immortal Spark

That which is life, the life of the life of every creature—God's command, the divine spark—never dies nor experiences change. It is constant and immortal. The body, on the other hand, is a compound mixture of elements, and will disintegrate.

Holy People

If God desires holy spirits, He suffices with the hosts of angels, *serafim*, and celestial creatures. What He really wants is human beings who hallow the everyday: He wants people who can withstand the enticements of the material existence, and strive for higher goals. God guarantees that you will reach your goal if you persist indefatigably. Be ready, because you may be the one who will get there, and will place the crown on the king's head.

The Real World?

In the material world it seems to us that the limbs of the human body are the reality, and the "limbs" of the soul an allegory. But in the immortal world of the spirit, the soul is the reality, and the body is but an allegory. By observing the 613 commandments, we get strength and rise higher in holiness—even to the level of Moses, who was able to remain atop Mount Sinai without food or drink forty days and forty nights.

4

Beyond Limitations

As Holy as Angels

Angels are spiritual and holy, and we humans can never hope to be like them. Still, God placed a small bit of pure holiness into every created thing, and that bit is as holy as any angel. With it we can raise the spiritual level of our body and of our life.

Unfortunately, because of our attention to physical pursuits, we forget our spiritual portion, and are the poorer for it. Were we attentive to our spirit, we could accomplish things beyond our dreams. No challenge would be insurmountable. Even if we feel successful, imagine how much more so we could be with our spirit!

The Infinite Spirit

There is a great difference between man's work and the work of God. Man takes a tablet and carves images on it; his work cannot be bigger than the space on the tablet. But when God forms an image, it is bigger than the material it was formed with.

Each created thing is made of both its material and its form, or spiritual essence. God placed a spark, a bit of spirit, into each creation. And while the material is limited and confined in an envelope of space and time, the spirit is not. The spirit is anytime and anywhere. It is without limit, and eternal. Regardless how limited one may be, regardless how challenged he may be physically, his spirit is boundless. Its energy is infinite. If energy is needed, it is at man's disposal.

This idea can best be illustrated by atomic energy. Wise men have discovered that the energy within the minutest bits of matter is awesomely larger than the size of the matter. The energy within the creation is infinite! When we learn how to release it, the results are nearly unbelievable. The Torah has the formula for uncovering the spiritual energy within, and those who are connected to it lead a life far superior to and elevated above the ordinary.

Spiritual Offspring

What spiritual offspring has man on earth? Man has within him a spiritual essence which is at once minuscule and infinitely big. His task is to focus on this spark and to help it spread throughout his physical life. If he can accomplish this, then every situation in his life becomes one of his offspring: they become imbued with the spirituality of God. But the only way to do this is by totally humbling one's physical life to the spirit. When the physical is negated to the Godly spark, the spirit dominates. Thus, offspring are begotten.

Therefore, before any deed is done, one must completely negate oneself to God. We therefore recite, according to Kabalistic tradition, "For the sake of the unification of the Holy One Blessed be His Name and His *Shechina*, to unify God's name, the *yod* and the *heh*, and the *vov* and the *heh*." In this way all our energies are focused on the spiritual energy within, and our deed becomes our offspring.

Beyond Healing

When one is ill and parts of him are not functioning properly, one is not totally happy. But one can be ill and get healed. The bacteria or virus that attacked one can be destroyed, and one's body can return to normal. This is also true on a spiritual level: man sins and defiles his spiritual purity, then he regrets his misdeeds, and with *teshuvah* returns to God with all his heart. His spiritual well-being returns.

In the physical realm healing is followed by scar tissue: the body does not return to the same state as before its illness. How then does the spirit return to its original state? It must reach beyond the world of nature, where the past and future merge. There it is healed and returns to perfection, as if it was never damaged. Then every part of it, now in a perfect state, is filled with joy.

True Freedom

The spiritual, which is the inner core of all creatures, is infinite and without limit. Therefore, the fact that the creatures have limitations is a condition forced upon them: it is due to their physical nature. By negating themselves to the Master of the world, they can overcome their limitations. The truth is, however, that all creatures are free without bounds or limits.

There is no greater blessing than to be free of all domination, and no worse curse than being a slave. This is one of the central teachings of the Jewish people, and is expressed in their severe opposition to the worship of idols or any other spiritual forces. Those are forms of slavery, and most miserable states for mankind.

We must always be mindful of our activities and make sure that they do not enslave us. We must be free to serve the One who created us.

Is Energy Limited?

One ought to think about one's energy this way: each person has a finite amount of energy, granted by God. If we waste it, we have less with which to pursue spiritual, meaningful, and constructive goals. We mustn't delude ourselves and think that we have limitless energy, space, and time. All of these are precious resources that are not replenished.

However, those who use their energy for the good, who risk everything to do the will of God, have their energy miraculously replenished, and can continue to do great deeds without limit.

Our Inheritance

The Jewish people at their very inception, starting with our forefather Abraham, were bound to God by a covenant. The covenant allowed that neither he nor his descendants would be limited by the natural world, but would be raised above it. Just as Abraham performed deeds of valor hardly to be expected from a human being, his descendants are able to act thus, too.

We must realize that even though we spare no effort to accomplish our goals, our efforts are still minuscule compared to our inheritance from our forefathers. It is more the energy of our inheritance that gets us over impossible hurdles, than anything we do. Therefore even after our persistent effort, we must not take credit for the accomplishment. The credit goes to our ancestors, who risked their lives for us.

Rising above Mistakes

As our life passes day by day, without doubt we will make mistakes. There isn't any person who is perfect or who cannot improve. Therefore everyone needs to repair those parts of their life that they have lived wrongly.

Since repairing is a human activity, imperfection again dominates. How then will man ever repair all his mistakes? By abandoning all desire for the self, and focusing on the Creator, man rises above his physical limitations and repairs all his misdeeds. He must risk all to rise above the natural world. Then, in one sweep, everything is repaired.

Good and Evil

The lusts of the physical world exist in contrast to the good deeds of the *tzaddik*, the righteous. His choice is manifest all the more when there is evil around him, just as we greet the sovereigns of other nations to contrast their false honor to the true honor which our kings deserve. We are also taught to say, "We would like to eat the meat of the swine,

but are prohibited by the command of God," again, for contrast. Thus the evil realm exists in order to help distinguish
the good.

Love and Secrets

The root of everything spiritual is infinite, and the closer we
get to it the more it is revealed to us. To get to the roots of
the mitzvos, the commandments, we need to observe them
with love. With fear of God, we would only skim the surface. It would prevent us from delving deeper into the roots
of the commandments: we would merely perform the command in its exact required manner, more performance than
substance. The love of God, however, inspires us to seek the
word of God within the mitzvah. The word of God is infinite, constantly revealing deeper and deeper secrets.

Small, yet Infinite

The physical world is as an illusion: a building which is on
fire. Although we still see the building, it is nevertheless
totally enveloped in fire. It is there, but how can we ever
hope to benefit from it? Still, God wants us to use the material world as a means of attaining its spiritual roots. By
negating our lust for its material aspect, and devoting ourselves to the spirit within, we raise its spiritual level.

The Jewish people as a whole, too, first have to serve God
within the natural framework, under the influence of natural
laws and astrological forces. But after they struggle in the
natural setting, and live spiritual lives, God lifts them up
beyond laws and limitations. They enter the realm of the
infinite beyond the influence of stars and planets. Thus they
are compared to the stars, which seem tiny when viewed

from earth but are actually enormously huge. So too, the Jewish people seem tiny in the world of nature by their actual number and estimated power, but in truth are even bigger than the world itself.

Our Spirit Is Indestructible

God planted a tiny bit of holiness into each Jewish heart which He guards with a vengeance lest it fade. No matter what sort of tempest or adversary comes along, that holiness will not diminish: rather, it will withstand all opposition. As the prophet said, even if all waters attempt to wash you away, they will not be able; even if fire attempts to destroy you, you will not get burned. The bit of spirituality is indestructible, and with its strength Jews in all the ages have gone on the pyre of the enemy with unfailing faith in their hearts as the fire destroyed their body.

The Eye of the Needle

There is the limited and microscopic mind of the human being, and there is the infinite and macroscopic mind of God. Man's understanding is but an entrance into the infinite understanding to follow. It is but the eye of a needle compared to the great light which is waiting to enter him from heaven. Man needs only to prepare the needle's eye through which the light of God shall enter his mind.

Higher and Higher

Each of us must constantly strive to attain higher and higher spiritual levels. This can only be done by wresting oneself from habit. By moving away from the world of natural laws, cause-and-effect, and habit, we can acquire new levels. Once we reach a particular level of goodness it, too, unfortunately becomes habit. We must therefore break out from that, too. And thus we constantly renew and blaze new trails in the service of God, and rise higher and higher.

A Doorway to the World Beyond

The universe is structured so that the deeds of man shall influence all of it. It depends on man's choosing: if he chooses life and good deeds, then the universe is uplifted to the realm of life and goodness, too; but if he chooses death and wicked deeds, then he plunges the entire universe into the abyss of death and wickedness. But inasmuch as everything is dependent on man, he only opens the door to that greater realm. He is not the prime mover of all that occurs. He merely produces, by his deeds, the tiniest of openings which connect the lower realm of creation, where we live, to the upper realm of the spiritual universe.

Thus although the accomplishments of man, especially in the latter part of the twentieth century, might seem overwhelming and awesome, they are still but tiny doorways that communicate with the upper realms. Therefore, we mustn't ever be too impressed with our greatness.

They Paved the Way

In any person's lifetime one can experience a variety of hardships. It takes great courage and strength of character to stay on course and continue toward one's goal. But thanks to our forefathers, who literally threw their personal life aside to do the will of God and triumphed, we too have the strength. They broke through all the barriers for us; all we need do is connect to their resolve, and we too are suddenly catapulted to the other side of the barrier. What we thought were insurmountable barriers suddenly melt away with the power of the will. But even though the path has already been made, each of us travels a distance according to his abilities. Those who negate themselves to our forefathers and their sacrificing ways can reach destinations beyond their strength.

Miracles

There are some people who observe God's commandments when it is convenient, but the Jewish nation as a whole has learned from its forefathers Abraham, Isaac, and Jacob, that regardless of the circumstances—beyond human limits, even when "impossible"—they will follow God's commandments. We remember that Abraham adhered to his faith in the one and only God in face of death in the fiery furnace of Nimrod. Isaac put aside all human emotion and walked with his father as a sacrificial lamb. Jacob brought up a faithful family against all odds in the house of Laban. Because they were willing to do the "impossible," God also did the impossible for them, and responded to them with miracles.

When all is dark, when there is no natural solution to the dilemma of the Jewish nation, God's miracles come to redeem it.

Beyond Human Endurance

The Ten Commands with which God created the world continue to sustain it to this very day. Similarly, the Ten

Tests of Abraham, which he endured with superhuman strength, continue to strengthen his descendants, the Jewish people. They are also the source of miracles which occur in dire need and rescue the Jewish people. After all, miracles are merely events beyond human experience. They are the reflection of the perseverance that Abraham had to fulfill the will of God, beyond the normal reach of human ability.

The Channel of the Fourth Dimension

Human beings are stuck in the material world of space and time. They are stuck in the present of that time: they can neither jump ahead to see the future nor go back to fix the past. God's gift to the Jewish people is to not be bound by natural boundaries: He gave them a channel through which they can see the future, and a path of repentance with which to fix the past. The path is available at all times, whenever they make the effort to use it. Although it is available to other nations too, for them it is limited to exceptional circumstances.

Other peoples need drastic change to remove themselves from the physical and fall into a trance or a dreamlike state, to move into the fourth dimension. The Jewish people, on the other hand, can go about their daily chores and still prophesy.

A Leap beyond Limitation

Although the kingdom of God is concealed in the physical world, it is revealed from time to time. In the Torah, which God gave us, His kingdom is always revealed. Therefore those who study the Torah can experience the presence of

God with clarity. Prayer, on the other hand, is our connection to God from time to time: we only have it because of our yearning for God. Our yearning is as if our soul wants to jump out of our concealed and limited state, to the infinite and revealed. That cannot happen on a steady basis, only from time to time.

Infinite Expansion

God created the world with ten commands. The creation was expanding to infinity until God said, "Stop!" That exclamation made the world as we know it possible. But the command, the voice inside every creation, is still infinite. That voice is the "voice of Jacob," and has an infinite quality.

The commands were infinite and spread laterally from a central point. When a Jew reacts to God's command, the "voice of Jacob" within, he is able to release the "Stop!" command and allow it to expand to infinity. This allows the command to take hold in the material world, expanding vertically into a third dimension.

Freedom or Enslavement

God grants to His servants absolute and unconditional free will, while others become attached, entangled, and enslaved to the laws of nature. The more one accepts the yoke of God's laws, the Torah, the less he has of the yoke of enslavement.

Similarly there are the six work days and the Sabbath. If God's rest day is esteemed, then the enslavement of the work days is lessened. Likewise, the welfare of the Jewish people among the nations depends on their acceptance of their role

as servants of God. And even one individual can add to the
freedom of the nation—or even the world, for that matter—
by humbling himself before God.

Even There

Even in the remotest, most obscure, illogical, irrelevant,
insignificant, inferior, and negligible place, the presence of
God exists and can be found. Therefore do not say, "How
can I, how will I, ever find God in this forsaken place?"
There is no place forsaken of God, and He is everywhere to
be found.

No Fear

Before one descends into a deep pit, one needs to fasten
oneself with strong ropes. If one is securely fastened, one
has nothing to fear.

Similarly, if we are totally connected to our Creator, we
have nothing to fear from any place or time.

No Place Is Too Far

Normally, if obstacles are in our way we must overcome
them. Regardless of the size of the obstacle, we will overcome it if our will is strong enough. Even if a place is very
far away and there seems no chance of ever reaching it, the
place will be reached if our desire is strong enough.

Similarly, some places are more conducive to feeling the
spirit of God, while others seem empty of God's spirit: but
even in those, with great desire, God can be found—just as
in the darkness we would not expect to find light, yet with
faith, hope, and prayer, light will be found. This is precisely

the sanctity of the evening prayer. It is a prayer of faith and a challenge to the impossible. We pray our way through the impossible, and find light even in the darkness.

The Forces of Nature

The everyday world, with its commerce, materialistic pursuits, longings, and lusts, is sometimes a danger to those loyal to God and His Torah. With all those forces tugging at the resolve of God's servants, how could they ever hope to remain faithful? Normally, it would be nearly impossible. But servants of God are forever giving up their life for His sake, discarding their physical life: their attachment to this world means nothing to them. Therefore the forces of nature have no power over them, and do not affect them whatsoever. On the contrary, God's servants have power over nature.

Timeless Israel

All mundane, earthly matters have their time. They are enveloped by and exist within time and the limitations of the natural order. But the Jewish people, as the chosen nation of God, are beyond and outside time. They are eternal, not affected by the forces of history. They have survived a hundred attempts at their total annihilation. They are, in a word, the light of the world.

In Each Heart

Each human heart contains all sorts of ideas about and solutions to spiritual problems. What one must do is work hard to find and uncover them. When one does, they will

be beyond all expectations. They will be creative strategies
to maximize one's potential and to help one to live a truly
spiritual life.

Near and Far

God is the furthest from mankind, nothing is further than
He; yet He is also the closest to mankind, and nothing is as
close as He.

Beyond Human Ability

Every human being receives a personal spiritual garment.
These garments do not necessarily respond to the lusts and
yearnings of the world; they protect man and help him live
a spiritual life. But there are powerful lusts—for power,
honor, and jealousy—that penetrate even those garments.
It is as if the person is suddenly without protection, naked,
and in imminent danger. How can one survive in times of
such great temptation? Only with the kindness of God, who
quickly clothes him in protective garments and snatches
him from the jaws of evil.

The *tzaddik* should not expect to save himself by his own
righteousness in all situations. Some situations are beyond
human self-control. It is then that God will come to his aid
and help him do what is humanly not possible.

Belief in the Infinite

Each creation is finite: in using it, we are locked within its
limits. We are anxious and worry about these limits. Will
there be enough? Will we be able to handle it? These limits

cause us pain, but if we are connected to the divine spark in all things, we are not limited by things. On the contrary, we are face to face with the infinite spirit of God. We realize then that the limitation was only on the surface. The inner reality was infinite.

That is the essence of faith: to stay steadfastly connected to the divine spark in all things. Then we never forget God.

Counting without Numbers

The stars are without number, infinite. Just as God created the universe ex nihilo, "from nothing" something, so too God numbers the stars, although they have no number.

The spiritual world is the one without numbers, and it is infused into the material world of numbers to bring light into the darkness. Similarly, the Jewish people are likened to the stars, infinite and without number. They are sent into the lands of numbers to teach righteousness.

Key to Infinity

The command "*Shadai!*" halted the expansion of the universe. Then the Torah was given and it released nature from the prison of finiteness. It allowed infinity.

The soul too is infinite, while the body is finite and keeps it imprisoned. Thus we need the Torah to set our souls free: with Torah our souls soar to heights unattainable.

Big and Small Mind

God's name *Shadai*, signifying "finitude," is the vessel in which the infinite providence of *Yod*-and-*Heh*-*Vav*-and-*Heh* can be contained. Therefore tefilin has the infinite name of God on the inside, and on the outside has the *shin*, signifying the name *Shadai*. The tefilin boxes are, so to speak, the vessels for the infinite spirituality of God. Similarly, whence a baby gets its milk has a small hole to channel the life-giving fluids to her with measure. The containing and confining of the infinite within vessels is called *mo-chin d'katnus*, "small-mindedness": big intellect, yet contained within a small physical brain. The Torah, however, is the opposite. It is the intellect itself without confinement: it expands and breaks through the boundaries and vessels. It is great-mindedness, *mo-chin d'gadlus*, allowing man to live beyond boundaries.

The Light Barrier

For every bit of light there is a bit of darkness. Therefore, as we advance to higher enlightenment we should expect to pass through darkness. It is like a jet plane flying through the air: the faster it flies, the more resistance there is, till it reaches a point where resistance seems at its maximum. That is the sound barrier. If it gets through that, it is beyond the barrier—and what an awesome experience it is! Similarly, when we encounter resistance as we attain higher and higher spiritual levels, we must move through it. When we do, we will experience a light which we never thought existed on earth. We will be beyond limitation.

To Share Oneself

The strength of the individual is to be someone in his own right, yet to venture forth and share with the community.

Similarly, the strength of the tribe is to have a distinct culture and civilization, and yet to venture forth and share those gifts with the world at large. That is the strength of the Jewish people. It is why they are finite in number yet have no number. They are one of the smallest nations, yet their numbers are connected to the infinity of God. Therefore they are also without number, as if they were infinite. And they are.

Above Limitations

The physical world, with its boundaries and limitations, is finite. Each creation can be found somewhere and sometime within its boundaries. Neither can a thing be everywhere, nor can it last forever. On the other hand, the spiritual world is infinite, and can be found anywhere and anytime. God placed a bit of this infinite spirituality into each creation. It is the soul of each thing.

Man has an infinite soul, for which he needs a vessel. He can help receive his soul by not allowing thoughts of limitations to bother him. He must assume that there are no limitations, as is true of his soul.

We get this strength from the Torah, whose words are bigger than the world. Those who study the Torah, or connect to its commandments, rise above limitations and accomplish great things.

5

The Light Within

The Light Within

In each created thing there is a light from the Torah that helps us find our way. We must work hard to find that bit of light; and when we do, we must toil to reveal it, to see it and learn from it. Our job, then, is to look for the light inside each thing we encounter, *daily*. If we don't easily find it, we need to try harder until we do.

Witness to the Creator

Nature grinds on monotonously, so that after a while we don't even take notice of its marvels. Every creature is made of endless wonders which point to its Creator, yet those go unnoticed by all except the few who care to look below the surface, the wise men who ponder the works of God and discover their awesome secrets.

Thus all creations bear witness to their Creator in their inner cores. But they are silent and no one would ever hear their statements; it is only the Jewish nation, with the Torah as our guide, who point out and bring attention to those witnesses. We are blessed with the sensitivity to hear the voice of every creature. The other nations ask that we please be their ears and relate what we hear. Perhaps reluctantly now, but when the *Moshiach* comes they will openly beg us.

We are blessed with the ability to hear the voice of each creature, and we ought to use it in our own lives and share it with others. This will make us more aware of the role that God plays in the world and in our own lives.

God's Spark Within

There is the crust of the physical world, and the spiritual inner core. Man's physical being desires the purely physical exterior, while the Torah guides him toward the inner spirituality. In addition, man has two angels: one, the *yetzer hatov*, desiring the good; the other, the *yetzer hora*, desiring evil. The *yetzer hora* has something to say about everything that man sees. It tells man to relate to the physical outer crust. At the same time, the *yetzer hatov* tells him to take another look and see the deeper, loftier, spiritual inside. Man is balanced as a quiver between these two inclinations, and has total freedom to choose one or the other. When he relates to the world as the Torah instructs him, he has won a small battle and gained mastery over a portion of his life.

For example, when taking hold of an apple, will a man relate to the outer crust and the purely physical, or will he relate to God's spark within the apple? This example can be substituted for each and every deed and relationship that man has on earth. By our choosing the way of the Torah, the *yetzer hora* becomes subjugated and vanquished, little by little, until we master our entire life.

Making the Spark Glow

On occasion we get a thought, a divine inspiration to do good deeds and live a virtuous life. Unassisted, that thought is destined to be extinguished, as a spark blown by the wind without anything to land on. We must take hold of that spark and dwell upon it, reorganizing our life around it by tuning out all other sounds and feelings. That small spark can brighten up our whole life and dominate our thoughts and deeds.

In the Presence of God

At times we experience fear, trembling, and awe arising from an unusual event. Because of the intensity of the experience, however, we are disconnected from it: we can't relate it to our life. We can look at the expanse of the Milky Way, with its millions of billions of stars, and be overwhelmed by its awesome vastness. Yet after we enter our home and resume our routine, there is no impact of our experience on our deeds. Similarly, fear and trembling before God, although spiritually meaningful, can be without impact on our actions and deeds. On the other hand, if we always behave as if standing in the presence of God, then our fear of God reaches maturity and becomes complete.

A Spark Containing All

A spiritual light descends and enters every created thing. In man too, there is an infinite heavenly spark that contains everything spiritual in concentrated form. Modern science is just beginning to understand how a minutely small entity can contain all the matter in the universe. *We* have always known this.

How can man connect his life to that holy spark? By totally subjugating his ego, his physical nature, to that higher reality. The body is incomplete and needy, replete with longing, lust, and the weaknesses of the flesh. It reaches completion by aspiring upward toward that holy spark. The heavenly light gives it infinite access to everything spiritual, and it becomes wholesome and complete.

Equanimity

The true servant of God is in a state of total equanimity at all times, regardless of the circumstances. Whether we find ourselves in poverty and hunger or wealth and abundance, our desires should be the same, focused on the ultimate outcome: to be near God and bask in His light. An illustration of this is the needle of a compass. When the casing of the compass is turned, the needle remains unaffected and continues pointing North: in fact, that is how a compass helps us find our way. If the needle shifted whenever we turned, we would soon be lost.

Those who point in a different direction with every circumstance soon lose their way; the true man of faith stays steady and firm. While circumstances churn around him, he is tranquil, grounded, and focused. He doesn't become the circumstance, but remains the servant of God.

Inner Light

A human being has a body and a soul. The body is a mixture of good and evil, while the soul is a spirit of infinite pure light. How do we elevate the body spiritually and have it shine with infinite light also? By seeking the light within the darkness, the spirit within the physical body.

By following the Torah and observing the commandments we discover the word of God within every cell of our body. That word is a light which is able to shine infinitely in all directions. The finite man is then able to influence mankind far beyond his physical capacity. It is the infinite spirit that is then active, and its influence is without limit.

To Bake Bread

Before man bakes bread, he must plow, plant, reap, thresh, grind, sift, and knead. Why is so much work necessary just to sustain man? It is a lesson from God to mankind: that from the most obscure of places man's sustenance can come. Who would imagine that from the earth bread could come forth? The earth seems to be without life: it is merely soil, dirt, a lifeless mineral! Yet when worked on and worked on, it yields food and sustenance. Similarly, we may wonder about some seemingly dead, fruitless aspect of our life. Can life ever come forth from there again? And we remember the bread from the earth.

All this is an allegory for the presence of God in all things. Where is God, and where can He be found? The answer is, wherever you look for Him: in the dew of the heavens and the fat of the earth, from the most lofty and heavenly to the lowest and most earthly.

Hidden Treasures

Do not be fooled or misled by the fact of man's creation from
the dust of the earth. He may very well be from the dust,
but he is likewise connected to heaven, as a ladder standing firmly on earth yet with its uppermost rung touching
the throne of God. Just as the earth is full of surprises, with
minerals, water, coal, iron, copper, gold, silver, salt, dia-
monds, and precious stones of every description hidden
within it, similarly, even in our ordinary physical life we
can find treasures of spirit. We need only work and look
below the surface, and we will find them.

Light in the Darkness

There is physical light and darkness, and similarly, spiritual
enlightenment and obscurity. However, even in the darkness God has placed light, as the light of the moon and stars.

Sometimes we are very fortunate and have a period of
light in our lives. It is then that we must store that light for
the days of darkness that may come. We ought not to take
it for granted and take no notice of it. We should cherish it
and keep it to help us live through our difficult moments.

That is God's gift to us before each of our life's challenges:
shining an intense light into our soul. With its strength we
grow with the challenge. The brilliance of that light is not
readily perceptible; we have to be sensitive to its presence
and take note of it.

Light for Truth

If one is locked in a dark dungeon, one can hardly see; but
had one infrared night-vision glasses, one would be able to

see everything. Similarly, if one is enslaved to an evil inclination, one feels nothing imperative about the truth. One would see again, however, if one observed God's commandments: those are the lamps and light for his eyes.

The Spirit within Lust

There are many levels of evil. Some are easily excluded from our life, and others are harder. There are basic lusts, however, that are almost impossible to avoid. The only way those are avoided is by our being connected to the divine spirit in each thing that we do: there is nothing then that we may do that is not divinely inspired. Only then can we be out of the reach of the illusions which entice us.

Flame and Light

In a flame there is the heavy burning gas of the heated material, and there is the light. One is the cause, the other the effect. With the light itself we can see from one end of the world to the other; that is what we ought to do.

Deep Glow

No matter what terribly oppressive prisons a Jew is thrown into, no matter what tortures his tormentors invent, the steady flame of faith will burn incessantly in the deepest depths of his heart. And its glow, although hidden from sight, will be sensed a thousand miles away.

Keepers of the Light

The nations of the world, ruled by the laws of nature and susceptible to its accidents, eventually cease to exist. They disappear from the face of the earth. What then happens to their treasures of wisdom and culture? They are absorbed for safekeeping among the eternal Jewish people, the nation of God. The Jews seek the divine sparks among the nations and give them a home in their spiritual life. Had it not been for them, those sparks would never be found again, as happened with great libraries of ancient Greece, consumed in flames and never seen again.

Heavy Loads

Our tasks in the world are many, and some are heavy and difficult. They weigh down on us, and we must carry their weight. We may even imagine them as a burden on our backs, as a donkey carrying a load; and those loads, as heavy as they are, make one think of the world as purely physical. It is drudgery, toil, and struggle.

Even in the most difficult circumstances one must remember the spark of divine light in all things. Even the backbreaking load has its roots in the light of God.

Reflected Light

Man's enlightenment comes in two forms. One is with a divine light that shines to him from heaven: it is a crystal-clear glass through which one can see all. The other is light which is caused by one's deeds: that is like a mirror, reflecting man's own image, and is imperfect.

One Morsel

In each morsel of food there is a kernel of divine light, a spark of spirit. It is from that that man lives, not from the physical portion, a fact observed by some nutritionists. Even one of these sparks would really be enough to give man sustenance and life. It is only because of man's shortcomings, his unrefined approach to life, that he needs to collect these sparks from many different foods and meals. If he would be worthy, one spark would suffice.

Reaching the Highest

The root of the life and existence of each created thing is in God, and the ones who can reach out and connect to that are the Jewish people. Therefore they can always experience God in all things. They can be uplifted to the highest levels and experience the miraculous.

Deep in the Heart

Each spiritual level we attain must be planted in the deepest depths of our hearts. There, within us, it will remain eternally, and influence us forever.

6

The Torah

The Direct Route

Each mitzvah in the Torah helps you reach the purpose of your being, to get close to God and connect with the root of your soul. So why search all your life on paths leading nowhere, when you can take the direct route? What would you rather do when you go from place to place? Of course you would rather get to your destination directly without detours. Do the same for your spiritual life.

The Real Power

God created the world by looking in the Torah. Therefore, the world has power over those who do not live according to the Torah. On the other hand, those who live according to the Torah have power over the world.

A Kinder World

The world was created with strict judgment. One aspect of this is the natural law, exact and unerring. But the laws of nature have a drawback. All natural things are impermanent—that, too, is a law of nature.

On the other hand, the virtue of loving-kindness is on a higher plane than the laws of nature. With it, the world receives longevity and permanence.

Love and kindness are the ways of the Torah, and those who are connected to its ways find a kinder world. But for those who turn away from the Torah, only strict judgment remains.

A Portion in the Torah

Each Jew has his own particular portion in the Torah. He will either find it during his lifetime, or perhaps he never will. The work that one does to find it is also particular to each Jew; what works for one may not work for the other. Yet that does not excuse anyone from working as hard as they can to attain it.

Diligence

Those who work hard and study the Torah with diligence, though they cannot understand it fully, God will help complete their plans. One should never become discouraged or despondent. No matter how difficult it may seem to understand the laws of the Torah, with diligence they will become clear.

Torah: The Source

The world was created with the Torah, and there is no place which is empty of it. Therefore there is also nothing in the world which opposes the Torah. The essence of the Torah, however, was given to the Jewish nation at Mount Sinai.

The Torah is the life source of all, and is like a brook whose waters never end. The water that comes from the source is sweet and gives life. Just as one who follows a stream ultimately arrives at its source, similarly if we follow anything long enough we will trace it back to the Torah. Even the other nations: when they convert to Judaism, become *geirim*, "proselytes," and trace their path—find their way—back to the Torah.

Purity and Impurity

The soul is from heaven and is pure, while the body is of the earth and a mixture of good and evil, just as the earth was desolate and bare. It is only through the Torah that the confusion of good and evil can be sifted and corrected.

The Letters of the Torah

The letters and the words of the Torah are the spiritual stuff from which everything lives: their very vitality. One of those letters is within each and every item of creation, and gives it its spiritual essence.

In our daily life we use objects, work with animals, and relate to human beings. After a while we get tired and bored of them; then we no longer treat them the way we did when they were fresh and new, and we were seeing them for the first time. How can we regain the freshness and pristine quality of the world? By connecting the things around us to their letters in the Torah. We then experience the unblemished spiritual vitality within them, new and fresh as ever.

Before we are born, we are completely dependent on the kindness of God, who sustains us in our mother's womb. The truth is, though, that after birth we are also completely dependent on God. Only we have forgotten. The more we grow and age, the more independent we think we are. Therefore we always need to readjust our sights, and remember our dependency upon God. When we do, we are as a newborn babe, reconnected to the source of life.

God's Infinite Desire

God created the world with His pure will, and desires it even now every instant. Thus our life, even this instant, depends on God's desire.

If we are aware of this we come to realize that our limitations are only imagined. What could stand in the way of God's desire? Thus every member of the Jewish nation can accomplish great things, even if they seem impossible. Similarly, if the divine desire keeps us alive, then we must tune in to it. We must negate our desire to His desire, the source of our being.

To serve God properly is beyond human capabilities. When one desires to serve God, his heart fills with energy beyond human strength.

How are we ever able to serve God? By negating our entire being to His desire, thereby receiving superhuman strength. We leap out of our limited physical life up into the realm of the divine. And then all limitations melt away, and the miraculous is nearby.

Above the Natural

There is the physical world and the laws of nature, and there is the spiritual world and the miraculous. There is the routine and expected, and there is also the unexpected. God gave us a vehicle with which we can tune in and connect to the miraculous: it is the Torah, the embodiment of the spiritual world. He who connects with it breaks loose from the fetters of limitation.

The inner light of the Torah is totally incongruous with the limitations of the physical world. It can only be grasped by those who do not heed limitations and are not frightened by obstacles. When one's heart opens to the possibility of breaking out of the chains of the physical world, one can also enter the infinity of the Torah world.

Maturity

Each creature was created in its maturity and completeness. Therefore even today it can strive throughout its life span to reach that selfsame maturity. Of mankind it is the Jewish people, with the help of the Torah, who can reach that original level. When they do, the nations of the world will revere them and receive spirituality through them.

From this, one realizes the great responsibility one has, not only for oneself, but indirectly for the entire world.

Rebuilding the World

God desired to create the world: therefore everything in the world has the desire of God in it. Whatever one looks at, one must think, "This is something that God desires." Studying the Torah can help us perceive God's desire in all things, and bring the world to perfection. Even if it is physically destroyed, as the Holy Temple was, we can still rebuild it on a spiritual level with the Torah.

When we learn Torah, we are rebuilding the world in the spiritual realm: when enough of that happens, the physical reflection of it will also appear.

Declaring the Unity of God

The value of a declarative statement does not depend on its power over an audience, but on how close it is to the facts. Therefore, when the nations of the world declare that God is one, it is not as valuable as when the Jewish nation makes the same declaration, because the Jews have the Torah, the word of God, as a guide. Their declarations are backed by their familiarity with the subject: thus they have the gift of speech.

If our speech is so worthwhile and important, we ought to reevaluate how we use it. We should use it more for revealing God's kingdom in the world.

Our Deeds Are God's Name

The entire Torah is a message from God to the Jewish people. It reveals His kingdom, and is therefore composed of His names in a variety of permutations. Therefore, when we follow the commandments of the Torah, the name of God is a seal on our deeds. The deeds are our offspring: we do them, yet they are the names of God—they emanate from Him. This makes good deeds even more similar to offspring, where the father, mother, and God are partners in formation. So too in the performance of good deeds: the deed is done through the medium of the person's body; his movements are a vessel to bring the good deed into the world; God and the Torah are partners in it.

Just imagine: we are merely vessels for the desire of God to reveal His kingdom. How much credit can we take for the acts of kindness that we do? We owe thanks and appreciation to God for the privilege to do them.

God Loves the Jewish People

God loves the creation and loves the Jewish people more than anyone. He gave them a letter, the Torah, lovingly relating the secrets of the universe, including a code of conduct. Each mitzvah that we do gives us spiritual merit, while each offense brings impurity. Unfortunately, the offenses are not only wrong, but have the power to extinguish the spiritual sparks gained by the mitzvos. As heavier weights on one side of a scale nullify the weight on the other side, so an offense on one side cancels a mitzvah on the other.

The love generated by the Torah cannot be extinguished by offenses. It is synonymous with God's relationship to the Jewish people, which is eternal. Athough they themselves are sinful and are surrounded by the sinful nations of the world, still God's love for them is intact. Not only is the love not extinguished, but it grows stronger. Just as we notice that when water is thrown on fire it bubbles, hisses, makes a lot of noise, and turns to vapor, and then the fire seems to burn brighter than before, so too, with the love of God for the Jewish people: when their merit is in danger of being extinguished, the opposition soon vanishes, and the love becomes stronger than ever.

The Torah Unites Body and Soul

Each person is physical and spiritual: he is two parts of one whole. By connecting his physical life to that of his soul, he becomes complete. He can accomplish this with the spiritual energy of the Torah; although it is from beyond the natural world, it reaches down to this world. It is a code made in heaven with instructions for our life, and can therefore unite heaven and earth, body and soul.

Being Close to God

Humans relate to the Creator on two levels. Every creature, man included, can negate its being to its creator. After all, what is a creature before its maker? Nothing. Therefore all nations—in fact, all mankind—can relate to the one and only God. Hence not only the Jewish people, but all men, have the prohibition against idol worship.

The Jewish people also negate themselves to, and worship no one but, God. In addition, though, they connect to the spiritual by observing God's commandments. This is possible because of their particular closeness to God. They need to be very mindful of their actions, and therefore have 613 commandments to guide them. The other nations, who don't share in this responsibility, do not need all of the commandments.

The Road to Life

Each human being journeys on a road his entire life. Where will the road lead him? He chooses this constantly. Therefore God, in His infinite kindness, showed man the road that leads to life both in this world and the world to come, and it is the Torah.

The Spark of the Torah

The Torah is from the highest spiritual realm and cannot be fully revealed. But from time to time in an individual's life, a spark of it is revealed. If he cleaves to that spark as the source of his life, then that tiny light becomes infinitely magnified. To the degree that one leaves the darkness, such will be one's power of cleaving to the spark of the Torah.

Torah in a Man's Heart

By contemplating the world of nature one can uncover the caring and love that God has for the creation. Such understanding is from the outer portion of the heart. Yet such revelation is not nearly as powerful as that of the Torah, which comes from heaven into man's heart. That is higher than natural understanding and beyond human capacity.

God's Love Is Greater than the Universe

There are two types of love that God has for the Jewish people. One is that He loves us as much as the entire universe. The other is even greater, and is called the greater love. It is greater than even the universe. The universe is only a creation of God and is therefore the lesser mind, while the realm beyond the universe is the major mind.

This can be compared to one who is faced with a task and thinks of his limitations. That is small-mindedness: he is limited by his own mind. But if he sets no limit and is ready to accomplish it in a great way, that is big-mindedness. Similarly, God's love for us is not even limited by the universe and the boundaries of natural laws. It is beyond everything known and experienced, as evidenced by the survival of the Jewish people against statistics and probabilities.

One Continuous Odyssey

Man is constantly on the move both physically and spiritually. Those who serve God with their heart and soul do not rest for a moment, but continually strive to move higher and higher. They don't miss a step nor any opportunity to keep moving: even if they are interrupted, they continue from where they left off as if nothing had happened. Suppose they are in deep study and devotion all day long, and then go to sleep: when they awake they immediately continue moving up in the direction they were going when they left off. Hours add up to days, days into weeks, weeks into months, and years pass; but the servant of God passes spiritually upward in one smooth motion his entire life—as if he reached out at birth toward the stars and at the moment of death is about to attain his goal. His lifetime odyssey is complete.

The Light of God's Commandments

God's commandments are obeyed with our physical bodies. The roots of God's commandments, however, are in the highest of spiritual places. How then does the spirit of the commandments connect with us? It is their light, their spiritual energy, which connects to us. But there are commandments which are merely in the mind, merely in man's will and desire, requiring no action. How do those find a connection to our material life? Only in the deepest and most sublime way, in the region of intelligence. There even the roots of the commandments are somewhat connected.

Thus if we gather our thoughts and purify our intentions and devotion before we perform a mitzvah, then with affirmation and action we connect every aspect of our physical being to the light of the commandments.

Love and Fear

There are two distinct qualities of matter: one is its ability to combine with other matter, the uniting quality; the other is its tendency to remain intact and distinct. For example, atoms of one element are able to combine with atoms of another element; on the other hand, the atomic structure of each element is such that it will remain as its unique self forever. The combining quality is love; the distinctive quality is fear. Oxygen is ready to combine with metals to make rust. This indicates that love can lead to falsehood, the loss of integrity and personal purity. On the other hand, fear protects the individual from combining with harmful elements.

In order to grow we need both the qualities of fear (to guard our integrity) and love (to reach out and produce new combinations). These two qualities are the spiritual core of the written law and the oral law. The former is akin to fear, guarding the integrity of each word and letter of the Torah. The latter is akin to love, reaching out to find new combinations of the law.

Obstacle to the Future

There is the written law, Torah Sheh'bichtav, and the oral law, Torah Sheh'baal'peh. The written law is for the here and now, the present life and circumstance of every Jew. The oral law is the transmission of the Torah to future generations. While the written law is a blessing, the oral law is a prayer: that our teachings guide the lives of the next and future generations. That is the place where the evil sets itself, as a rock on the mouth of a well, so that the wellsprings no longer give to drink. It is an obstacle to both our prayers and our strength in transmitting the Law. Yet it can be overcome.

The Private Torah

The entire Torah, God's teaching, was given to the Jewish people. Each person, however, has his particular teaching, a specific goal for his life, and it is concealed within his soul. When that particular teaching is brought out into the world, he has reached the truth of his being.

Dark Matter

Darkness is the absence of light, but at its root it is dark matter, the inclination to do evil. God keeps the two opposites, light and darkness, away from each other. That keeps the light and darkness in their original form.

There is a light, however, that can negate dark matter, evil itself. That is the Torah, whose light is so brilliant that it totally wipes away dark matter.

Busy with Torah

When one is busy all day long with Torah study and observing mitzvos, the light of his soul will light his way and will feel the deepest redemption.

Torah and Prayer

There are two types of people, just as there were two types of trees in the Garden of Eden. One type is like the Tree of Life, unchanging and constant in his holiness. He is unimpressed by evil and unshaken by challenges of faith. The second type is like the Tree of Knowledge, confused and a mixture of good and evil. To overcome each new challenge he must be helped by God: otherwise he succumbs.

Similarly, there is Torah study and prayer. Torah is the Tree of Life, and prayer is the Tree of Knowledge. The roots of Torah are from the eternal world, the way the world ought to be, while the roots of prayer are from the confused good-and-evil of this world. Through Torah we connect to eternity, and through prayer we beg for help in the here and now.

Channels for Torah

The Torah is the word of God and far removed and out of reach. Man must prepare vessels, channels in which the wisdom of the Torah flows from the eternal springs to mankind; but really each person creates his own vessels and his own channels as he works to refine his character and habits.

The Torah's Protection

The nature of exile is that God's kingdom is concealed. We can hope to reveal it to some degree, but never completely. How then can we deal with evil, the cause of concealment? We can take protection in the Torah, which is likened to water covering the fish and protecting them from "evil eyes." And just as the fish hunger for every new drop of water, we too, by hungering for every new word of Torah, will find safety in its protective waters.

New Hearts

Just as the physical world is recreated every day, so is the heart of man. The world gets its renewal from the ten commands of the creation and the heart gets its renewal from the Ten Commandments of the Torah. If one connects his heart to the Torah, it is constantly renewed.

History of the Future

In the divine realm there is no past, present, or future: it is all one and the same in complete union. Thus the very Torah that the Jewish people will receive because they longed for it is the Torah that attracted them, the future in the past. And the longing that they had for it is the longing in the Torah that attracts them to it, the past in the future. It is all in the present, whether longing for it or not, it is all there in the Torah, both the history of the Jewish people and her future. It calls to us, it entices and calls to us; it wakes our hearts to come forth and be part of the Torah which we are already part of, in the future.

We Need the Torah

The righteous, because of their highly developed spirit, find the divine within nature, the light within the darkness. Ordinary people like us need the Torah, which comes from the highest realm.

Digesting Knowledge

Our digestive system starts with our mouth. We masticate our food, breaking it into tiny pieces. From there it mixes with chemicals, and dozens of processes break it into its chemical components. Finally the nutrients are absorbed into the blood, and they feed and revitalize the cells. The roughage, refuse, and unusable part of the food is eliminated. In illness, when the body dysfunctions, refuse remains in the body and can lead to danger: the body cannot tolerate unrefined material.

Similarly, in the realm of the intellect and the spirit man must carefully break apart and analyze what comes his way. He must carefully choose which parts he will ingest and hold dear, and which he will discard. The Jewish people in their host countries must do the same. They must deal carefully with the culture of their host and only adopt that which bears letters of the Torah. Their souls cannot tolerate unrefined ideas.

Total Attention

In order to hear words of Torah, divine teachings, a man must disregard all distractions: he must not turn to any earthly event calling his attention. He must focus on listening to the divine message, then he will hear it.

Understanding

Wisdom is like seeing: we can see from afar. Mentally we can conceptualize a thing, but we really don't understand it—it is still at a distance from us. Understanding, however, comes from proximity: we must be near and related to a thing in order to understand it.

Light of God's Name

The Torah has many words and the name of God appears interspersed throughout. Those names light up the text and make it divine. Similarly, the soul of man lights up the many words which compose his body.

More Important than Life?

The life of man is his most important commodity; he desires that above all else. The Torah, however, teaches that there is something even more important than life: the word of God. Before the word of God, our life is worthless. We have no direction, and all of our efforts can result in nothing: a total waste. A waste of all our ancestors preceding us, including our parents. A waste of our mother's pregnancy and birthing, and the efforts put into our upbringing. A waste of all the meals, work, exercise, and travails of entire lifetimes: a total waste.

God's word has to be prior to man's understanding, too. After he hears the word, he can reason and deduce what the meaning is.

God's Path

The Torah is the "path" which God had, so to speak, chosen for Himself. And therefore it is the very best for us, too.

Torah of Kindness

The Torah is like a queen who has a guard in front and in back of her. One must guard and observe the commandments of the Torah with strictness, if he plans to connect to the Torah. The Torah is purely loving-kindness, and a human prone to lying and wickedness cannot connect to it. If he is worthy to receive the Torah, if he studies and is immersed in it, then he must be on guard again, lest he fall into the trap of arrogance. He mustn't think, "Oh, how greater I am than the others!": on the contrary, he should dwell on the kindness of God that has allowed him to study and understand the Torah. He will then be filled with shame: "Why am I worthy to study the Torah, when all these people worthier than I cannot?" Then he will repent from his erring ways, and realize his modest accomplishments.

To Think like the Torah

The more a man subjects his desires and will to the Torah, the more he merits that his logic coincide with the Torah.

Laws of the Torah

A despot and dictator doesn't listen to or observe his own laws and decrees: he is the boss and no one can tell him what to do. On the other hand, God, the master and ruler of heaven and earth, "observes" His own laws. They are identical to the laws of the heavens and the earth. Similarly, the Jewish people in observing the laws of the Torah can cause the natural world to reflect the laws of the Torah.

The Roots of the Laws

Not only did the Jewish people receive the laws of the Torah, they also received the capacity to fathom the very roots of those laws, to be able to climb higher and reach the names of God which compose the Torah. Those who understand the roots of the laws are able to compare and contrast them, and to derive one law from another.

Between Man and Man

There are commandments dealing with the relationship of man and God, and others dealing with man's relationship to man. Although rooted in social mores and civilization, they too, are equally God's laws from Sinai. By behaving with the utmost care toward mankind, one is able to understand the Torah laws even deeper; the more he understands them, the more respect he has for mankind. This spiral continues upward without end.

Divine Justice

Although the nations understand the laws of the Torah, they adopt them as their own. The Jewish people, however, always consider them as God's laws, and negate themselves to divine will—a feat hardly possible in a position of power.

Although the Jewish people practice justice and mercy, it is attributed to God. Everyone sees and is witness that the justice is not "Jewish": rather, it is divine.

Therefore, any judge who wishes to work with divine guidance and insight must subject his wisdom and being to the divine will. Then the light of Sinai will shine forth from him with a glimpse of God's justice.

Open Ears

To a man who does not listen to the laws of the Torah we say, "What do you need ears for, if you don't use them to listen to the Torah?" On the other hand, God opens the ears of a man who yearns and strives to grow in Torah knowledge and observance each day, enabling him to listen and understand the deepest secrets of the Torah. Even if he naturally has difficulty understanding, is learning disabled and mentally challenged, nevertheless his ears open and he suddenly understands the laws of the Torah.

Preparing to Receive

The preparation before receiving the Torah is as much part of the Torah as the Torah itself; and the end result, the Torah, helps the person during his preparation.

Being a Mensch

The Torah makes a man a more compassionate human being, which in turn enables him to more deeply understand the Torah, and to be even more of a mensch. The manner of that mensch will in turn be more and more holy: divine light will glow from his deeds.

The goal is not to be holy, however. What is being holy? Where is there a place in this world for that? The goal is to be hallowed through holy deeds and observing the Torah. It is through them that man receives garments which are always more and more holy.

The Deepest Well

By observing the laws between man and man, we increase civilization and multiply peace and harmony throughout mankind. That peace is the well from wherein one can draw the deepest understanding of the Torah.

The Torah Lifts Up

Even if the person is inadequate, the Torah itself lifts he who dwells on it, striving to understand and judge with its laws. Not so the nations, who have laws but do not bring more understanding to those who use them in judgment.

Accepting the Torah

By accepting the Torah the Jewish people accepted divine guidance and dominion. Being servants of the Most High, they understand His laws and are able to grow in Torah all the time.

One Letter of the Torah

Just as every cell in the human body carries the entire blueprint for its structure in its chromosomes, genes, and DNA, so too each letter of the Torah comprises the entire Torah. Although it is incomprehensible, each letter is a unified singularity: not only are the five Books of Moses a unified singularity with one message, not only are the six orders of Mishna and all the tractates of the Talmud one singular message, but they are so definitely singular that all of the Torah is in any one letter. Thus the Jewish people, in cleaving to the Torah, become united in the highest spiritual way. Any one Jew is the entire nation, and the entire nation is really one singular Jew.

In this we are different than all the other nations. If one Jew is in trouble, all of the tribe of Israel is in trouble. Not because of our empathy to another: one Jew is not merely another, he is the entire tribe.

Torah Light

The light of the Torah makes it seem as if the world is light. One can think, "It is light, I can see!" while it is not. The Torah is light, but the world is not: it is full of darkness. We need to hold the light of the Torah deep in our hearts, and walk into the world of darkness with its glow to light our way.

Power of Commandments

There is a separate commandment to spiritually uplift each of the limbs and parts of our body. There are some so powerful though, that even one can uplift the entire body to a higher spiritual level.

Out of Reach

The Torah itself is totally out of human reach, higher than the angels. It descended to the level of the Ten Commandments so the Jewish people could receive it, and descended further to the level of laws between man and man. We need to spread the Torah even further into all of nature, till there is no place without Torah.

Laws from Heaven

Although we may understand some of the Commandments logically, we must observe them only because they were commanded by God. Therefore, even if the non-Jewish court makes judgments with identical laws as the Jewish one, we may not adjudicate our cases with them, because our laws have nothing to do with theirs. God gave us our laws, and they, copying ours, made up theirs: they are not the same.

Where Is Truth?

This world is full of lies, wickedness, and quarreling. It is not pure truth. Had it been perfect, it could not exist: it would have disappeared in the true existence of the One and Only Creator. Where can those who seek truth on earth find it? It is in the Torah given on Sinai. One who wishes to have truth, righteousness, and peace must work very hard to attain them. He is going against the stream, and has a mighty battle at hand, but if he fights for it he will get there: the Torah itself will help him get there.

Servants Need Parables

Animals and trees, birds and beasts, can teach us how to serve God. These may be used as parables for our lives, as the industriousness of the ants, the strength of the lion, the lightness of the eagle; all of them can teach us an aspect of

God's service. But when we receive the Torah and observe its commandments we no longer need parables. That path is higher than nature, and brings us directly before God.

It is like a son and a servant of a king. The servant does the king's bidding, while the son is a member of the royal family. When the son obeys the king, he safeguards the integrity of the family. He does not need the same explanations or logic to convince him. He does it for the same reason as his father bade it, and in the same spirit that the king had desired it.

7

Humility

Our Prayers

When we pray to God for help, the words and letters themselves help us to humble our being before Him, and to depend on Him wholeheartedly.

True Humility

The more an arrogant person receives from God, the more arrogant he becomes. On the other hand, the humble person feels less and less deserving each time he receives. It defies man's very nature to become more and more humble because of God's gifts.

It is as if a guest were placed at the table furthest from the dais at a dinner: there he was expectedly humble, thinking himself neither deserving nor honored. Then the host moved him closer to the dais, and he became more humble. He kept thinking, "I am so undeserving. It is embarrassing that I am being moved among the notables." Then he was moved to table after table, until he was finally placed at the dais; and still he remained just as humble as when he sat in the back. That true humility is very unusual.

God's Gifts

If a man becomes arrogant on account of God's gifts, it is because he feels full and no longer in need. On the other hand, the righteous humble themselves and always consider themselves lacking, and he who is lacking is an empty vessel and again ready to receive God's gifts.

There is another aspect to this. The wicked are rewarded for their good deeds with gifts: they therefore become arrogant and boast of their merit. The righteous, on the other hand, do God's service for His sake, not for rewards—therefore they do not feel deserving. Neither does God reward them because of their deeds: He rewards them unreservedly, purely as a gift. Therefore, not only should the righteous feel humble when they receive God's gifts, but they must realize that it really is so. They do not get anything as compensation, but merely as a pure gift.

The Undeserving

When one human says to another, "I am undeserving," he may still be arrogant and boastful. He really means to say, "You know how deserving I am, and by saying that I am undeserving, you offer me more honor." But one who says to God, "I am undeserving," realizes that as a creature he has no merit, and is a nothing and a nobody compared with God's majesty.

Therefore God subtracts from the reward of those who think they are deserving of God's gifts. But the righteous, who know that whatever they receive is an undeserved gift, will not have their rewards subtracted from by God.

The Deer's Skin

The deer has very tight skin, and it is constantly "jumping out of its skin," reaching beyond its tightness, and speeding along. Therefore we are admonished to be as the deer, speeding to do God's will.

In man this tight skin is his physical body, which is limited in space and time. The soul in him is infinite and yearns to expand beyond the body. In fact, the yearning and longing to attain higher spirituality is caused by the soul's incarceration: that yearning is at the root of all service of God. The more the righteous rise in spirituality, the less room there is within their body to contain that spirit, so they "jump out of their skin" to have more.

This is the deepest meaning of humility—when man feels too small to contain the gifts of God, which are given in great abundance. He feels as a vessel being stuffed with one hundred times as much material as there is room for. "Me?" one asks, "How could all of this be for me? Look how tiny I am compared to all these gifts!" That is true humility!

Higher than Animals?

Do not think that just because man's brain is more complex and rules over the world, he is higher than the animals. Generally he is higher, but there is a spiritual aspect in which the animal is higher. An animal accepts his fate in total resignation without thinking, while man practices much thinking.

This is also true of the righteous. The closer a man is to God, the more he subjugates himself in His presence: therefore, the closer a man is to God, the more he is like an animal, without a brain or will of his own but to do the will of the Master. Now who is higher, man or animal?

God's Delight

God delights in His creatures. Even those who are rebellious and antagonistic to God's ways have some moment in their lives when God delights in them. Just as the more a creature shows that it is owned by its master, the more its master delights in it. Similarly, the more man reveals God's kingdom, showing who the master is and who is the creature, the more God delights in him.

The Wall

Humbling oneself is the greatest and truest of wisdom; thinking of one's own wisdom as the greatest is plain foolishness. When a man is humble, he can perceive the word of God with such force that it seems to be an impregnable wall. Nothing can penetrate it nor vault over it. The fool, on the other hand, has no sense, and bends his mind to whichever way the wind is blowing.

Errant Servants

The name for the Jewish people is *Yehudah*, spelled yod-heh-vav-dalet-heh. Except for the letter dalet, those are the four letters of the tetragrammaton, the name of God, spelled but never pronounced. What can we learn from this name? It is clear from this name that God is always with the Jewish people—not because we are deserving, but because we are poor: we are the least populous of nations. That is the letter dalet in *Yehudah*, meaning "poor." We really have nothing, therefore God gives us everything. In fact, God gives everything only to him who has nothing by his own merit.

The Messiah will be everything for the Jewish people, and therefore he will be from a tribe whose origin and history are tainted with nothingness. Judah had children from his daughter-in-law, thinking she was a harlot; his descendant David had children from Bat Sheva, a woman who was considered married at the time. The redemption sprouts forth from the dalet, the poor erring servant of God, and not from Joseph's tribe, who were righteous throughout. Who can follow in their footsteps? David makes room for every member of the tribe, even those who are nothing.

Ready to Call God

The Jewish people have learned from their forefathers to call out to God whenever they are in trouble: this readiness, the humility of helplessness, is the stance which gets an answer from God.

The Empty Vessel

In order for a man to receive from God, there should not be any barrier. One must rather be the most perfect and complete vessel, and lower himself to the very earth, to the dust, to be completely empty and ready to receive. The ones who can do that to the utmost are the Jewish people, who were

sent to earth from heaven to be the channels for God's blessing. They do this by being nothing but vessels for God's gifts.

Peace is Shalom, a name ascribed to God, and only He
can give it to mankind. In that process God's presence enters
mankind, and we must be completely empty in order to
receive it. Therefore the sages say: "Open for God an opening the size of a needle's eye, and I will open for you doors
large enough for a palace." One must be the hole in a needle,
nothing and empty; then he can receive God's blessing.

The Other Side

The spiritual world after death is a reflection of our life.
When we live with the guidance of the Torah, observe the
commandments, search for the truth, and yearn for God's
presence, we prepare the same on the other side. Therefore,
whatever man does in this physical lifetime, he prepares a
copy of it on the other side.

True Humility

The righteous know the truth about human existence: we
are completely dependent on our Creator for our very life;
we are nothing and nobody without God. Therefore, there
is not even an iota of an impulse to rise and hold oneself
over and above another human being. Even when we rule
over others we know that the others are not lower than we
are. Could anyone be lower, more in need, more dependent
than we are?

This gift of true humility was given to the Jewish people.
If they desire, they can truthfully be the most humble of all
the nations. Although others will also seem to be humble,
it will be sheer falsehood in comparison.

8

The Righteous

Good Deeds

What is the biggest and most ultimate good deed that was ever done? It was the creation of the universe. No deed can match it.

We also know that the universe wasn't merely created, but is recreated all the time. Those who ignore this may do deeds that do no not enhance—but rather, destroy—the world. Those who are aware of this treat their deeds with more care: they want to enhance a world being created that very instant with their good deeds. Thus, if our deeds are connected to the biggest deed, we can truly call them *ma'asim tovim,* "good deeds."

The righteous want their deeds to be vitalized with God's energy, the same energy with which He created the world. As they do, they are totally subjected to the source of all deeds. Their deeds are done in the purest way, and every bit of them enhances the creation.

The Inner Essence

God created the world; but many deny its divine origin because it is a mixture of good and evil. They see the false, the impermanent. The righteous person, on the other hand, looks for the divine particle, the spiritual essence, in all creations. He does not deal with the physical part of the world exclusively: thus he bears witness that God created the world. Because he does this, he awakens the spiritual spark which is in each creation. As a result others are also able to see the spiritual within the created world.

Our Covenant with God

Two people who sacredly share a common thing have a bond and covenant with each other. They guard this bond with an oath, and even with their very life. The creation also has an inner part, a spiritual essence, that is sacredly shared with God. When creatures guard this spiritual essence, they are upholding a holy covenant between God and the world. On the other hand, when creatures only consider their physical outer part, they neglect the covenant and bring disgrace upon God's name.

If a man guards the covenant, it follows logically that God will give him life. It makes sense that God will keep the spiritual essence in him: after all, he respects and cherishes his inner nature. But when man neglects his spirit and disgraces the covenant, then we are puzzled: why is that man alive? The same is true with a nation or the entire creation.

If they don't bring respect to God's name, then everyone wonders: why do they exist?

The righteous *tzaddikim*, those who guard the covenant, answer this question by bringing honor to God's name. They are the foundation of the world; they place the world on a solid foundation. When people see the deeds of a *tzaddik*, they understand why God created the world.

A Dwelling for God

With his good deeds, a righteous person builds a dwelling-place for himself in the world to come, the spiritual realm. Similarly, he builds a dwelling-place for God in this world. Thus the *tzaddik* has two dwelling-places: one in this world, and one in the spiritual world. His task is to unite these two dwelling-places so that they are one and the same, that his life in this world may match his spiritual life in the world to come.

The *Tzaddik*: Beacon of Light

It is a sad fact that people sometimes lapse into pure physical indulgence. When this happens to a nation, its deeds are soon forgotten, and its entire culture is in danger of disappearing; this has happened numerous times in the history of mankind. Fortunately, from time to time a beacon of light appears and sets humanity back on the path of God. That beacon enlightens mankind, making them aware of the consequences of their pursuits, and by example directs them.

This is also the intention of every *tzaddik*. By realizing his responsibility to the world at large, his example shows others how to live a truly spiritual life. He helps people and nations not to disappear: thus he is the foundation of the world.

Two Types of *Tzaddikim*

There are two types of righteous people. There is the *tzaddik* who wants to do what's right, but needs God to make it possible for him; and there is the *tzaddik* who totally negates his being, with *mesiras nefesh*, throws his life to the side, hurls caution to the wind, and finds a way to do the will of God.

Fears No One but God

A man who fears only God is the happiest and has the least-troubled look on his face. He is calm in his confident knowledge that all that happens to him is a direct command from the Creator. Therefore sins, lusts, barriers to holiness, are a mere joke to him. They make him laugh. Who could be afraid of those things? There is one and only one to fear, and He is God.

On the other hand the wicked—who fear all physical dangers, who are affected by every human emotion, whose lust is unquenchable—laugh off the seriousness of sin. Why do they laugh? They pretend that the power of the idols, lust and emotion, has no power over them. But the opposite is true: they succumb to every wind that blows at their frailties. By contrast, the *tzaddik*, the righteous one, is firm and unmovable in his faith.

The Work of the *Tzaddik*

The work of the righteous is to bring holiness into the everyday, to perform the acts of civilization—commerce, shelter, sustenance, procreation—in a spiritual manner. Before he attempts to do that, however, he himself must be free of evil and materialistic confusion. His mind and body have to be hallowed by the avoidance of purely materialistic pursuits: then he is able to guide others in relating to the world. But if the *tzaddik*'s own life is full of confusion and struggle, how can he bring clarity and holiness to others?

Unity

The righteous one seeks to unify while the wicked are rending asunder. The *tzaddik* builds while the wicked destroys. Yet we sometimes see that the wicked gather and are unified; that unity is only so they can better destroy and divide. They use that positive energy for evil.

With all of mankind being so different and diverse, what is the factor that unites them? It is the holy sparks, the bits of divine spirituality that are in every item of creation. The *tzaddik* looks for them, finds them, loves and cherishes them. He sees the common denominator, the core and inner life of each thing, and relates to it. Everything is the same to him in that aspect; he sees the inner holiness in every man. The wicked, on the other hand, focus on the differences, the outer portion of all things. Their relationship with them sets them apart and ultimately leads to their destruction.

The *tzaddik* seeks and collects holy sparks even from the wicked, and thus lives a hallowed life.

Calm in the Storm

The wicked have no foundation and no place, and therefore in a storm they are totally lost and in peril. The righteous *tzaddik*, on the other hand, has roots in and lives in the presence of God. He is calm not only when the storm approaches, but also in the very midst of the storm.

This is like a pregnant woman who is running away from her pregnancy: wherever she runs the fetus runs with her. The thing to do is find the help of God within the trouble itself, the medicine that can be extracted from the wound itself (as has been done with vaccines, where the infective agent yields a protective serum).

Therefore, when one is in trouble he should not run away from the trouble: it might just run with him. He should rather find relief in the trouble itself.

The Many and the One

The *tzaddik* starts with the many—many talents, many devotions, many acquaintances—but he ends with unity: he unifies his talents, his desires, and his friends to reveal the kingdom of God. He starts with many but ends with the One. On the other hand, the wicked start with togetherness: they band together, gather their ammunition and forces, but in the end fall apart and go their separate ways. They start with one, but end with many.

World in Balance

The universe expanded from absolute unity level by level, shell by shell, till God said, *Dai*, "Enough!" It was expanding into plurality bit by bit, and was nearly very materialistic; just at the right balance, before it reached the point of no return, God said, "Enough!" Thus the *tzaddikim*, the righteous, can still redeem it: it is not lost beyond repair. The wicked, who rejoice merely in the physical world, nearly tip the balance. They may keep the world in darkness, but the righteous work hard to lift the lower levels and unify them shell by shell, till all the world is one.

Waiting and Thanking

When the *tzaddik* is redeemed from exile, he affirms his faith that all his future exiles will end in redemption. Thus he always waits for good things to happen. He not only waits, but thanks God for the future help which he has not yet received.

Both Are Righteous

There are two types of *tzaddikim*, "righteous persons." One effortlessly sails through life, continually gathering higher and higher elevations of spirituality. Then there is the other, who is confronted with challenge after challenge, tempted by wickedness, dishonesty, and corruption. He struggles with them all and walks away victorious. Both guide us and show us the way.

Paths

There are currents in the ocean, in the deep and on the surface of the water. There are also currents of air, paths through the forests, and roads traversing the globe. They are there with purpose, and are waiting for spiritual adventure. Those who are spiritually sensitive can feel the longing of the paths to fulfill their missions. The righteous also are sensitive to the spiritual tasks inherent in all things and in all moments. They can sense the importance of meeting another human being, and the potential of the moment. In a word, they are tuned-in to the eternal.

Moses and Abraham

Moses brought the Torah from the heavens to the earth. He delivered the path of miracles, of revealed providence. In contrast, our forefathers brought the earth to the heavens. They lifted the mundane material world and sanctified it. They stubbornly stood to uncover the truth in the face of wicked opposition, and to establish God's kingdom in every circumstance.

Always Ready

Although the Jewish people may fall into the abyss of sin, even idol worship, they are still ready to sacrifice their lives for God. In every exile it is the oppressive hand of the enemy that keeps their hearts distanced from Him; as soon as the oppression ends they are back in God's service in full force.

God Helps even the Wicked

No one, not the wicked nor the righteous, can finish the work they start. It is only the power and energy of God that helps them conclude. It is a balanced scale: when the materialistic stoneheartedness is removed from the righteous, the wicked start to exhibit it. The sparks of light fly from one to the other, and they are enveloped in darkness. Thus the more the righteous shine with good deeds, the more obscure are the dark deeds of the wicked.

Dry Land

The entire creation is witness that God created the world. While others witness in silence, man is the only creature who can communicate with complex speech. His witnessing is of the highest order. The places that man inhabits, all the lands, the cradles of civilization, are where the witnessing takes place: if it doesn't, shouldn't it be washed away with a flood? If man is a witness, should not he be able to declare it everywhere, even in midst of the sea?

The Bubbling Brook

The goal of the *tzaddik*, the "righteous," is to raise everything to the level of divine spirit. The vitality in minerals feeds the vegetative forms, vegetation feeds the animal kingdom, and then man takes all of them and raises them to a divine level. He brings all of their vitality and spirituality home.

How is man able to accomplish this? Because his soul was breathed into him by God Himself, it is the bubbling of the brook of Life. Our life is the bubbling, and the source of it is the brook, the divine presence in the creation. Thus man takes everything and raises it to the level of his soul.

Deeds Lasting Forever

One can do a good deed, and it lasts a day. One can also do others that have a longer life, weeks, months, or even years. But there are especially major, deep, and intense deeds that may last even a whole lifetime; and in exceptional circumstances deeds can survive into the next generation, and perhaps change the course of history. This was accomplished with the ten tests of Abraham, which were progressively more difficult. The tenth one was finally so intense that it altered Jewish history forever. It gave the unique strength to his descendants to remain firm in the face of adversity, and that strength is with us forever in its fullness.

The Righteous

The natural world, having been created, is finite and lacks perfection. It is the *tzaddik* who, through his righteous deeds, takes the spiritual realm and connects it with the physical: and whatever is connected to the roots will not be lacking.

By being righteous, we not only repair our own life, but bring perfection to the rest of the creation.

Manner of Speech

God created the world with the twenty-two letters of the Hebrew alphabet. He is recognized by His "manner of speech," and so too is a *tzaddik*, a "righteous person," also recognized by his manner of speech. With those twenty-two letters the ten commands were said and the world was created. Unfortunately the words and letters of those commands were hidden in oblivion in the murkiness of the exile, evil, and wickedness of mankind. Among the Jewish people, however, they were preserved; and those very ones became the Ten Commandments, God's manner of speaking to His people. Thus by observing the Ten Commandments, the Jewish people uncover the ten commands and the twenty-two letters.

Letters in Food

The sustenance of all creatures is from the letters of the Torah embedded in the food they eat. Though he be fed, there is no satisfaction unless the creature is actually able to see those letters, the divine sparks in the food. Therefore a *tzaddik*, who looks within, finds satisfaction from the food he eats, while the wicked, who experience merely the outer crust, are always looking for more.

There Is Always Hope

The righteous are blessed and the wicked are cursed. Yet no matter how lost one is, how deeply mired in profanity, there is hope. By yearning constantly to do the will of God, thanking Him with deep appreciation for being able to serve Him, and believing with unshakable faith that doing God's will is the highest order of deed, such a man will move from the level of being cursed to that of being blessed.

9

Truth and Falsehood

Truth

Love and fear of God correspond to expansion and contraction. In love we expand the envelope of our caring to include others; in fear we contract that envelope. Neither of those two virtues by itself is spiritually pure. In love we have lust, and the loss of great amounts of energy amounting to nothing. In fear we have the falsehood of inaction. But if we combine the two, to love with contraction and focus, that is truth.

Eternal Truth

Truth never ceases to be true, and is eternal. Falsehood, on the other hand, has a limit, ends, and is no more.

Truth in a World of Lies

God's seal, His very essence, is truth, and the degree that one is connected to Him determines how close one can get to truth. Because this world is full of lies, deceit, deception, and trickery, it is nearly impossible to be truthful to the fullest extent; but if we use the holy book of truth, the Torah, to guide our life, we can hope to live with truth.

The Charm of Falsehood

God is the one and only, and is truth. Plurality, on the other hand, is falsehood. This plurality is merely an illusion. What we see before us with physical eyes is the outer portion, the shell of what is within: inside, at the core, all things are spirit and holy sparks. There is unity at the inner core of all things.

From where does the shell get the energy to fool us? Why does it have the power to charm us into thinking that it is the truth? Why are people fooled by plurality? It is because we continue to value the shell, the outside of things. We are enthralled with packaging, and it therefore charms and fools us. The power of evil over us is a projection of our minds: we look at it as powerful, and our mental energy gives it power over us. With the advent of the Messiah, however, plurality will cease, and all creatures will recognize the unity in all things and all people.

Dots of Truth

There is sometimes such a small difference between truth and falsehood that adding one little dot (period) or a line (comma) would change a statement from truth to lie. The righteous know the importance of a dot, as the tiny spiritual speck which is in them, their soul. They cherish that more than anything, and it will remain everlastingly: it is eternal. Therefore, they will not trade one dot, one iota of truth, for one dot of falsehood.

Ashamed of the Truth?

How will we ever face God at the moment of truth after we die? Will we not be ashamed of the inescapable truth? Will we not be ashamed of the puny number of good deeds we bring with us?

On a deeper level this means that God's presence is merely concealed in nature. It is really everywhere, and we are in its presence. When we are in trouble, we are really with God—yet we behave as if God is nowhere around, and we therefore are afraid and complain. Suppose God were to reveal himself to us: would we not then be ashamed?

By our risking everything and sticking tenaciously to our faith, the truth is revealed and obscurity changes to enlightenment. It is then revealed to us that what we believed was really true: God was there all the time, and we have nothing to be ashamed of after all.

Man and His Garments

One's inner core, the soul, is pure and unchanging. The things that change are the external circumstances in one's life: they are the garments which change from environment to environment. Still, they should not affect one's inner spirit. One should always be conscious of the fact that the soul is in God's presence at all times. It never leaves His presence, and neither should we ever forget our Creator. We should also behave with the knowledge that we are in His presence, regardless of external circumstances. We should know who we are, regardless of the style or kind of clothing we wear.

Truth or Exile

The truth is that God is everywhere. What we experience in exile, an eclipse of God, is false. Thus, in order to survive in exile we need the virtue of truth. The stronger one is connected to truth, the less effect the exile has on him.

The End of Falsehood

Truth is eternal, while falsehood is finite and must end: that is the secret of all exile. But to know that secret is also to know that all exile is merely an illusion: God's spirit is always there, even if hidden. We are in exile to learn and to teach that very truth, that God is everywhere and always to be found—that through the darkness, light will be uncovered. While some see this with the clarity of an unclouded lens, others may not. Although one does not see because of the dark exile, with faith he will live to see it with clarity.

Open and Closed Lips

The lips help us express our thoughts in clearly articulated speech. On the other hand, by closing they help us remain silent.

Truth within the Lie

Each divine spark, true and infinite, is surrounded on every side by falsehood, lies, and wickedness. When we see a gathering of evil, we might assume that there is no way that any truth could be present in that spot: it just couldn't be. Yet we can say assuredly that despite the predominant presence of evil, a kernel of truth must be there.

One example is the Germans during World War II. When we read and watch documentaries of their cruelty, bestiality, and total wickedness and evil, we could declare, "These are inhuman beasts, and there could be not one iota of a redeemable part to their story!" But then, look again! The Germans searched for any Jew, even those who merely had Jewish grandparents. That is a redeemable fact: it stated that no matter how far back in ancestry, one is still part of the nation of Israel. Being a Jew is special, not some coincidental title to be cast away at whim. Another truth, no matter how grim the consequences, is the plain fact that the Jewish people are indestructible. Even when the most powerful country in the world pooled all its logistical and military resources to accomplish the annihilation of the Jews, they failed. Another truth is that after the most horrible and crippling massacre in the annals of human history, the same Jewish people gathered and got back to the business of life as before. It is nearly incredible, and statistically close to impossible, for that to occur. But nevertheless it did.

There, plainly, is one big horrible evil lie, and in the midst of it are eternal truths. Who would ever guess?

To Reach the Truth

Each person will realize the truth according to the level of his faith. Even the most righteous *tzaddik* in the whole world will have some point of doubt where he must have faith: even he will not reach the truth unless he has faith.

Phantoms

Evil is like a shadow cast on the ground: it has no substance, and is merely an absence of light. Those who are tuned-in to God's truth see immediately that falsehood is merely a phantom and an illusion. They are not frightened by those imitations of reality.

Admitting the Truth

The word "to thank," *mo-deh*, and "to admit," as when one admits his sins and errors, *mo-deh*, are identical. When one is always thankful, he has the insight to admit that what he thought was unfortunate was really good, only his sight was obscured by physical longing and desire.

Truth of the Truth

Emes, aleph-mem-saf, is the word for "truth." Aleph is the first letter, mem is the middle letter, and saf is the last letter of the Hebrew alphabet. This means that truth is true from the beginning to the end. It is true through and through; there is no part of it—nothing preceding it and nothing coming after it—that contradicts its truth. The single letter which means "truth" is vav, a letter that grammatically changes a verb from the past tense to the future tense and from the future tense to the past tense. For example, *ye'hi* means "it will be," while *va-yehi* (adding a vav) means "and it was." *Ha'ya* means "and it was," while *ve-haya* (adding a vav) means "and it will be." The letter signifying truth turns the future to the past and the past to the future, because truth has no past or future as a separate entity: it is one indivisible truth. What was true yesterday, in the divine sense, will be true in the future. And what will be true, was already true.

This is the difference between when a human consoles another human, and when God consoles man. A human being can only deal with the present, and consoles the present; he cannot change the past miserable event which happened. But when the God of truth consoles us, He changes the tragic event into one that brings gladness. Although we are quite unable to understand this in a world where time flows in one direction, in the divine sphere it flows backwards and forwards. It is truth.

Preceding Truth

Every act which is preceded by the fear and awe of God is done in truth and with one's essence. When such an act is done it leads to a deeper fear and awe of God, and that itself is an indication of authenticity.

On the other hand, when an act lacks fear of God, it is not done with complete truthfulness, nor does it add to one's feeling of God's presence. Falsehood and deceit creep in and it is defiled and weak.

10

Exile and Redemption

Yearning for Eretz Israel

It is difficult and sometimes impossible to observe all of God's commandments in the exile. But that is all we can do, and it will suffice. We find the same contrast between two servants of God, one who does everything he is told, the other who is constantly prepared to do His will. He waits and yearns for more. The first will not be punished for always doing the correct thing, yet the second is greater for constantly striving to do more.

We will not be punished for meagerly observing the commandments in our exile. Still, those who yearn for the Messiah, to live in the Holy Land and observe all the commandments, are spiritually even higher.

Liberating

The soul is dressed in a material garment and is enslaved in its finiteness and limitations. We must work to liberate her and allow her to accomplish infinitely more.

In Exile

In every exile of the Jewish people, in every suffering of mankind, God too is in exile and is, so to speak, suffering. His creatures are in trouble, trouble brought about by His granting them freedom of choice and will. That causes Him much pain. He must do it, but would rather not, as a mother must sit by and watch her child take his first steps and hurt himself with many falls. Thus, when the righteous *tzaddik* prays for redemption, he prays for the divine exile to end, for God to enjoy His creatures. While he does that, he may even forget the earthly exile of his people.

In Orbit

When an object comes within the gravitational pull of a planet, it is attracted and moves in its direction. Man, too, when he gives up his illusion of independence, is attracted to God and moves in His direction.

Man can also be in exile, and prevented by oppression from moving in God's direction. As soon as he is ready, however, the obstacles disappear.

Predictions

Just as we need to tell of the miracles God did for our forefathers, so they needed to predict the miracles God will do for us now.

For Father's Sake

If a prince knows that he is leaving his father's palace to go to a land far away for his father's sake, he is not in exile. Otherwise, all the work he will do there will be a burden, and all tasks oppression and suffering.

Similarly, as soon as the Jewish people realize that they are spread throughout the world to bring honor to God's name, they are immediately released from exile, spiritually as well as physically.

No Repeats

If we remember that God can put us into a tight spot, and redeem us too, then we don't need to be put into that same tight spot. Whereas, if we forget God, and have the conceit to think that we are strong on our own, then God places us in a tight spot, again and again.

The Wheel

The word *goh-loh*, "exile," is also rooted in the word *gal*, and *galgal*, "a wheel." The wheel turns, and the part that you thought would never be on top is suddenly on top. Had it not turned, who knows if it would ever have moved anywhere.

Similarly, and unfortunately, some people's lives never change: not for the worse nor the better. The only hope of changing them is by turning them upside down. When they land and right themselves, they begin over and start anew.

Experience of Exile

There are three levels of individuals in exile. There are the
average people who are unable to actualize the holy spark
within them. Then there are the righteous, who are—in
their deeply spiritual awareness—not in exile at all: actually they are the cause and harbingers of the redemption.
And lastly there are the downtrodden who are in such bad
straits that they no longer feel their pain. Yet God redeems
them all with one blink of an eye, simultaneously and with
the same powerful sweep.

Civilization's End?

With each holy spark liberated by the Jewish people from
their host nation, what is left is progressively more materialistic and wicked. Cracks appear in the fabric of that society, and cultural fragmentation and degeneration ensue.
Because their exile gets worse and worse, the redemption
of the Jewish people is soon to follow.

The King and His People

There is no king without a people, and the more loyal the
Jewish people are and act as His people, the more the kingdom of God is uncovered. Their behavior has a great influence on the ingathering of the exiles.

Servants in Exile

If we accept God's kingdom as servants during the suppres-
sive exile, we will be worthy to be His children when the
redemption comes.

My Heart Is Awake

While a person sleeps his life and vitality is gathered in his heart, unable to spread into all his limbs. Similarly, the Jewish people in exile have their light in their deepest depth, and it cannot take hold of their real lives. That is the cause of great yearning.

They Can Redeem

The righteous who recognize that even within the exile there is God's mindfulness and providence bring redemption to others. Their faith is palpable to the wicked, who, smelling it from afar, run away.

Faith or Exile

Exile is the eclipse of God's presence. Those whose faith is unshaken by oppression are nearly not in exile.

Identity

The Jewish people are always afraid of their exile, lest they intermingle with the host nation and lose their national character. They are the chosen people, with an enormous responsibility for all of mankind. Therefore, God reassures them that no matter how horrid an exile they are in, their identity will never be erased.

Redemption

First all the spiritual "worlds" must be fixed and released from exile. Then the redemption will take place on earth, too.

The End of Oppression

There is no end to oppression, stress, and the pressures of life. But it is also true that one ought not allow himself to be oppressed, and stressed. That is spiritual enslavement. On the other hand, he who is a servant of the One Most High, is a slave to no one. To the degree that we subjugate our being, and recognize our total dependence on the Creator, so will we be free from other types of oppression.

The Solution

The task of the Jewish people is to reveal the kingdom of God. Most of the nations are opposed to them. Regardless of the intensity of their opposition, it will never exceed the ability of the Jewish people to overcome it: as the folk saying goes, "We will outlive them!" No matter the strength of the enemy, God will not forsake us. The Jewish people as a nation will always survive.

This is not so with the other nations. They can cause their own disappearance by their own blunders, as we have seen happen to several ancient and modern civilizations.

In this we learn an important lesson for our life. If one has a problem, the seed of the solution is there, too. Do not delve on the problem, but seek the solution from within.

Most Dangerous Places

A father can enter all the dangerous places and prepare a path for his children; and a father can also show his children the worst of all possible exiles, so that they will know that even there—God is.

The Cause of the Exile

Each of the exiles was caused by one of the cardinal sins: idolatry, incest, and murder. The fourth, our present exile, is caused by hatred without cause. The root cause of all four of them is dispersion and disunity: idolatry is contrary to the belief in a unified One God; incest is contrary to the sanctity and unity of family life; murder is contrary to respect and unity of people; and lastly, hatred is surely the opposite of unity.

On the spiritual level, all mankind needs to unite in the service of God. One who recognizes the importance of declaring God's kingdom will have only love and respect for anyone else who shares his goals. Thus, if we haven't the full measure of love for another human being, it is because we are lacking in our respect, awe, and love of our creator. The root of all exile, then, is the disunity between man and God. Redemption will come from seeking and being one with Him.

Even the Trouble

When the Jewish people are redeemed, they praise God and see His greatness. They also have to realize, though, that not only the redemption, but even the exile itself, was an act of God.

When an individual is ill and recovers, he is very happy and praises God for answering his prayers. He too has to realize, that the illness was an act of God, just as was his recovery.

Forced to Save Us

Our forefathers jumped into the most dangerous places to declare God's kingdom, and God was, so to speak, forced to save them, and thereby reveal His awesome power. We, the Jewish people, who follow in their footsteps, also are in exile after exile, in the cesspools of the world, and again God is "forced" to save us and reveal His miracles to mankind.

The Entire People

God promised to lift the Jewish people from the depths of exile to the pinnacle of redemption. That promise, however, was made to the Jewish people as a whole. In order for any individual to enjoy the fruit of that promise, he must first negate himself and become totally unified with the Jewish nation. Then he too is made part of it.

Clothing

A woman is mature and complete, and ready to fulfill her destiny and have children. The maturity can be recognized in her fully developed body. Still, she dresses and beautifies herself. That does not add to nor diminish from her completeness. It is all on the surface, not in the essence of her being.

Similarly, the Jewish people are the children of God, fully developed in the divine scheme, and are always connected to the Creator. Their garments, the manifest part of them in exile, are the problem: the Jews' oppression prevents them from acting as children of God. They can ignore their troubles and continue to serve God with devotion. Then their garments are noticed and admired. But their connection to God really does not change: they never leave God's presence.

Uncover the Darkness

There might have been two suns, one for the day and one for the night. The moon was made smaller though, to give light in the darkness, and the stars were added to amplify its light. The sun, a consuming fire, represents all the other nations, their light ruling the day, the material world; the moon, a mere reflection of light, represents the Jewish people, who light up the darkness; and each star is one individual: one more additional speck of light, lighting the darkness of the night. Therefore, the Hebrew word, both for "exile" and "uncover," is *goh-loh*: to be in exile in order to uncover the hidden kingdom of God; to penetrate the darkness in order to uncover the light.

In the Dungeons

A prison is not the place where thoughts of freedom are born. It is a place of hopelessness, futility, and despair. It is a sad place where one expects no change and nothing good. But what if you go to prison in order to uncover secrets for the king? What if you risk your life behind enemy lines in order to save the kingdom? Then you are there with hope, anticipating the sprouting of freedom.

The Jewish people have been trained to enter the darkest of darkness from the days of their forefathers. They do not forsake hope even in the most horrible prisons. They are there in the service of the King, and are happy to be the messengers and harbingers of hope of freedom.

Sparks Throughout

The tiny, yet spiritually mighty, sparks of divine light are spread throughout mankind. It is the task of Jewish people to gather them and make them all one. Then all mankind will realize that the light they had possessed was from the One and Only. For this the tribe of Israel is in exile, to search for, find, gather, and unite all the sparks and make them one.

11

Good and Evil

Knots of Evil

The knots which the wicked tie do not last. They are based on falsehood and have no foundation. On the other hand, with the commandments of the Torah a Jew can "tie" himself to the Creator; and through that tie one separates himself from evil and is free to serve God.

Celebration

When the wicked are punished in their afterlife, their parents are brought to look at their suffering. Contrarily, when the righteous celebrate, their parents are granted a visit and enjoy the celebration together with them.

The Power of Evil

God gives the power, freedom, and volition for every creature to do evil. Who but God can do that, give life to him
who rebels? When we are confronted with the utmost wickedness, we are frightened, lest we fall into its trap. We must
realize that the evil's power is granted by God Himself; and
God being there, why should we fear it? Thus we can calm
our fear and be confident that the evil will have no power
over us.

Why Evil?

Why is there suffering? Why is there evil? They are there
to make a difficult course, to force man to choose between
good and evil. He must not only choose, as two distinct
colors of black and white, but must separate an intermingled
mass of events and information. When he does, and sees
clearly which is good and which is bad, he reaches his goal:
he is enlightened and grows spiritually day by day.

When No One Listens

Even if no one is listening to the words of rebuke of the
leader, they should still be said. The words enter people's
hearts, and there lie dormant. Later, they are awakened and
bear their fruit.

Tolerance?

At times the oppression of exile is so severe and unrelent-
ing that we adjust, and defensively tolerate the worst treat-

ment. We tolerate the defilement and wickedness, not differently than New York citizens tolerate twenty-five murders a week in their city. Even for this we need God's mercy and blessing, that our souls should not become deadened to the vile ugliness of our host countries; that we should maintain a semblance of spirit, a spark of light within the darkness; and that we should be intolerant of wickedness, and pine for justice and mercy.

No Pain, No Gain

The creation of man was from the dust of the earth. As God was making him, he could not do nor say anything; he experienced great pain then, and finally, with God's breath filling his lungs, he spoke and was man. Similarly, when we enter the world through the birth canal, we experience great tightness and difficulty; we finally emerge, and utter our first sounds. And so on throughout life, if we are fortunate, we move through the constriction, the pain, and emerge more developed. Even our morning rising shares this element: we need to rise, yet we want to continue sleeping. We are pained by the necessity to get up and start our day, yet we move through that nap period and suddenly are able to get on with our work.

Banish Evil

God is never older, never old, but is always new every instant; and the spirit of God, which gives vitality to every created thing, keeps it fresh and new also. That is called the kingdom of God. Man is the creature who has the awareness of God as king and creator: therefore it is he who through his deeds can proclaim God's kingdom. With his faith and prayers, acknowledging God's sovereignty, he causes all creatures to feel God's rule and His fresh vitality.

If man would have unshaken faith, like an impregnable wall, then no wickedness or evil could affect him. But through cracks in the wall, and weakness in faith, evil is able to gain entry and influence mankind. Otherwise it has no strength on its own, and would wither away.

Full and Empty

Abstaining from evil deeds makes us vessels to receive blessing. Again, by emptying we become full, by being full we remain empty. There are also the heart and the eyes: when the heart is empty, it is full of prayer; when the eyes are empty of greed, they are full of generosity.

Both of these are the charm that the Jewish nation is blessed with. Their heart is constantly full of prayers for the entire universe, the family of man, and their own tribe, and their eyes are full of generosity for the blessings endowed others. They only want their own.

To Deny Darkness

Man's soul is the spark of God's holiness, and he has the power to draw everything within that holy circle. By his making that effort, all of creation is humbled at man's feet; if not, if man uses his enthusiasm, power, and yearning for evil, then he will see the entire world as merely darkness and evil. This is similar to when we don't like someone and we project that he hates us. Similarly, if we despise light and want it far away from us, we project that the light is escaping from us and despises us; just as the wicked, who reject God's ways, often think that the righteous ones hate them, while usually the opposite is true.

If, on the other hand, we tenaciously believe that there is light within the darkness, even if we are blind to see it, we nevertheless will see it.

To Forget Evil

The more man remembers evil, the more it remembers him, and he has to struggle with it. The more he forgets evil, evil forgets him too: then he remembers God, and is at peace.

Illusions Come to an End

The idea that the world is only its physical nature is merely an illusion, the darkness which covers the light. It is an illusion that, were it so, would be beyond redemption. Fortunately, it is not so.

Illusions have no place in the world, and are limited both in space and time. They really can't grow, and will come to an end. They can only grow in our minds as we allow them to cover the truth. When we forget God, darkness reigns; when we remember Him, we have light.

Attracted by Illusion

There is the inner truth, and the exterior illusion. The truth should be very important to us, while falsehood should be of minor importance. Yet, unfortunately, we are often misled by illusion and consider it as the most important thing in our life, as in love and lust. Surely lust is but a tempo-

rary and unimportant part of our relationship compared to
lasting love, respect, and growth.

A magician also entices his audience with illusions. He
only has power over them when they come close and stand
around to watch. What power have his illusions in the pri-
vacy of his own home, with no one watching? None. Illusion by itself is nonexistent and without the slightest power;
but if we are drawn to it by its charm, we are caught in its
net. Those who realize that the illusory part of their life is
totally unimportant will not be trapped by it: on the contrary, they will pass over it, walk away from it, and focus
on the truth.

Evil at the Gate

For every closing there is an opening, and for every opening a closing. Even when the gates of holiness open, there
is a closing, so that only those who are worthy enter. Thus
the closing, the tightness that we experience, is only the false
aspect of the truth. Really there is no tightness or obstruction—it is but the outer appearance, the lip and edge of the
whole. If we were privileged to see the entire truth, it would
be clear to us that the obstruction is but an illusion.

A Pit or a Well

The challenge of evil is like a deep well. A man can fall into
it and think he is in big trouble; but a well can be filled with
water, and it is then a source of life. Torah is the water with
which to fill the wells which come into our lives: then,
instead of pitfalls, we have wellsprings of cool delicious
water.

Illusion of Exile

All exile is merely an illusion. Were it clear to man that every challenge coming his way is from God, he would never think he is in exile. Yet how can we have that perception, and see beyond the pain and suffering? It is only with the power of prayer and Torah. By cleaving to God's teachings, and turning to Him for help, we can feel His presence even in the worst times.

Good and Evil

There is bad love, as lusting for the merely physical, and bad fear, as fearing objects or people. Then there is good love, as to love God, and good fear, as the fear of God. There is also in each of us the *yetzer*, the "desire to do good," and the desire to do evil, which are rooted in love and fear. The righteous one clears his heart and leaves it empty, as a pipe, a conduit for God's will; and just as when plaque accumulates on the inner walls of the heart's arteries, all sorts of debris get stuck there. When cleaned, through diet or an operation, then blood flows through it freely. It is the same with man's spiritual heart: when he focuses on illusion, illusion fills his heart; when he clears it, evil has no effect on him.

Strive to Improve

Every ordinary person tries to better himself. Thus, as he grows older, he improves by refraining from evil and increasing his good deeds. Each day leaves him with less and less evil and more and more good. If we could observe him

for the rest of his life, his highest spiritual moment would
be the last second of his life: that is when he would have
the least evil and the most good.

Not so the righteous. He does not wait till the end. He
strives to live the correct life right from the beginning.
Although he too is constantly improving, he is not reform-
ing. No need to drop bad behavior or evil deeds. All his
deeds are good and getting better and better.

New Challenges

Just as God renews the creation each and every day, the evil
also has renewal. Although you defeated yesterday's evil,
today you will struggle with a new, trickier one, with a
strange fresh strength.

There are two ways to defeat the ever-newly-born evil.
One is by observing the commandments, the mitzvos of
the Torah. The other is to separate oneself from evil completely and totally. With these two weapons evil can be
defeated.

Two Paths

There are two paths before man: one seems to be smooth,
but is thorny and difficult in the end; the other is thorny
and difficult in the beginning, but in the end it is smooth.
The former is the path of one who indulges in merely material pleasure. It seems easy and smooth, one need not
struggle with great obstacles in order to cross it; but in the
end, at the end of one's life, one is left with a very difficult
and suffering eternity. His soul has not attained purity and

holiness, and cannot enjoy the spiritual pleasure of God. Those who choose the other path, and struggle to gain spiritual heights, will reach a pleasant eternity.

There is another difference between the two lifestyles. Those who choose what seems to be a thorny path, and in the end reach "smooth" eternity, will realize that it was the other path which was really thorny, not their chosen one. On the other hand, those who choose the path which seems smooth, and reach a thorny eternity, will never realize their mistake. That is because they only realize their mistakes who struggle to reach enlightenment, but they who never struggle remain in their ignorance.

On the Tightrope

One who walks on a tightrope must constantly be vigilant and aware of where every inch of his body is. He continuously adjusts his weight to balance himself; he moves with total awareness, setting himself on the right course. It is as if he was continually getting on the rope and starting over and over and over again. Not so the tightrope walker who walks smugly and absentmindedly. Because of his ignorance or forgetfulness he fails to adjust to new conditions and circumstances, and may fall to the ground.

Similarly, man must be vigilant about evil forces which may upset him and throw him off the path of life. Thus he is forever starting anew, and renewing his efforts and dedication. Not so those who think they have nothing to fear: while they sleep, the forces of evil have already pushed them off the right course, and when they wake up they will see that all they have struggled for is in ruins.

Good Balancing Evil

The spiritual world is balanced, with good on one side and evil on the other side. We have three levels of spiritual energy inside of us: the spirit, the breath, and the soul. Juxtaposed opposite them are the three physical weaknesses of jealousy, lust, and honor. Jealousy is a result of not realizing the unity of all souls: a man is merely jealous of something that another facet of his soul has. Lust contradicts the breath of life which God put into us: how can we lust with our divine breath of life for things that also contain God's breath of life? And the desire for honor is ludicrous, considering that the spirit of man is destined to sit before God's Throne of Honor.

If we succumb to the three weaknesses, we lose our spiritual powers. If we work hard and overcome them, we are able to direct our physical life by the dictates of our Creator.

It Is Easier

It is easier to create a completely new world than to fix the destruction caused by the wicked.

The Tree of Life

When God placed Adam, the first man, in the Garden of Eden, some part of his soul was able to connect with the Tree of Life. After he sinned, that connection was hidden, to be revealed through acts of righteousness.

Each one of us, therefore, as he participates in being a *tzaddik*, experiences the connection to the Tree of Life; and when he does, he can see from one end of the world to the other.

Half and Half

For every creature that was created in the physical world, an angel was also created. Thus, every creature is only half; the other half is an angel. Similarly, man is also only half of his being. A complete man is half earthly and half an angel. Whatever happens to the creature on earth also happens to the angel in the spiritual world.

Thus man is connected to the spiritual world. His actions contribute to the well-being of the entire world, both physically and spiritually.

Now just think: what great things can be accomplished, or on the other hand destroyed, with one's deeds? How much more careful one would be if one would realize this. How much importance one would place on each of one's actions, and how careful one would be when one does it.

12

Free Will

If Not for Desire

There are the higher and more spiritual parts of creation, and the lower more materialistic physical universe. Of the two, the heavenly one is of course the more perfect. Then why the lower one at all? Because the creatures of the earth have desires, while the heavenly angels have none; and God has great joy from the desires of the earthly creatures, when they choose to do His will.

So just think: suppose you are in a dilemma whether to do the will of God or your own will. Suddenly you realize that the only reason you were created was to harness your desire to do God's will. What a precious choosing that is for the entire creation! How could you abandon the reason for your being, and follow the path of evil?

Wasted Gifts

God gives to each creature what it needs. His giving has no bounds and is without limit. To receive His blessings we open our hands. We can take and take, but unfortunately we lose all of it if we have no container; all God's gifts will go to waste if there is no vessel to hold them. How do we protect our talents and gifts from going to waste? We must envelop the gift and restrict its use from wasteful activities. We must guard them carefully: then we will surely have them.

Free Will

When man was created and looked at the world, it was obvious to him that the Creator was its master. There was no doubt whatsoever. Wherever he looked he saw God: there wasn't a place or happening in his life where he didn't see God. He hardly had any choice but to do the will of God, and because he saw God everywhere, he didn't need to work for his sustenance. He was in the Garden of Eden, a palace of all delights and a table set for a king.

When he ate from the Tree of Knowledge clarity ended, and in its place came obscurity. Although he could still see that God was the master, it required more effort. He suddenly was able to interpret things in more than one way. He was confused. He saw things happen but was able to attribute them to causes other than God's will. He then had to choose: to do God's will or to draw other conclusions.

Choice, free will, is our greatest attribute. It separates us from the instinctive actions of animals. Yet it is not our greatest glory. It came to us by an act which lacked faith:

eating from the Tree of Knowledge. Perhaps man wanted the volition to discover God and didn't want to find Him readily wherever he looked. Because he chose to work for it, he also chose to get lost on occasion.

Root of Man's Strength

Every physical creature has its root in the spiritual realm. Now if this is true of even the lowliest creature, then man, who is the crowning glory of the whole creation, must have powerful roots. He has great amounts of wisdom and will-power at his disposal. In fact, God put him in charge of the entire world to respect, cherish, and care for it. His superiority is a great blessing and he must be very careful not to waste it. To the degree that he guards it, that is how much he is replenished by his spiritual roots.

Man's Initiative

Every creature needs the assistance of God, but there is a difference. If man initiates an action through his own choice, then it has longevity. If God has to urge man to action then it does not last, because it did not grow out of man's being, but was placed into him by God.

One whose actions begin with his own initiative God helps to finish everything on his own; but he who is weak must be helped, and is helped all along.

Two Ways to Perceive God

There are two ways to find God. One is by contemplating the intricate nature of the universe, and recognizing that it

took an all-knowing God to create it. The other is by using
the inheritance which our forefathers have planted, as seeds
of faith, deeply in our hearts. Finding God the first way will
depend on our level of intelligence and understanding; finding Him through our inheritance, however, is not dependent on but beyond understanding, and beyond our limited intelligence.

Habits to the Task

A man may possess habits which are foreign to the worship
of God, and they may hold him back from serving God with
all his heart. But if man is constantly thinking and figuring
the best way to serve God, then he harnesses even his habits for the task.

Desire and Will

God's spirit is everywhere to be found, but it is hidden because of the wicked and the evil in the world. Were there
no wickedness, then His spirit would be always revealed;
were He revealed, there would be no wickedness. Therefore
there is a dichotomy, a separation between the earthly sphere
and that of the spiritual, because of the mixture of good and
evil on earth.

We hope and pray for the day when unity will reign and
both the earthly and spiritual spheres will be united without separation, when God's presence will be just as revealed
in the earthly sphere as in heaven.

There is plowing and reaping, to search for the hidden
and then to find it. There is desire, hidden in man's heart—
even unknown and unactualizable—and will, which is ac-

tive and in the open. Desire is earthly and in exile, and will is released from exile. These two will also be unified some day, and unity will reign both in a person's heart and the whole universe.

Before Thought

There are wicked surroundings that prevent noble thoughts and ideas from reaching the surface. Because there is evil all around him, one may never know that he is about to think a noble thought. Yet God knows, and with those seeds He is able to awaken man's soul to desire righteousness.

Not to Interrupt

One who is bitten by a snake and still does not interrupt his devotion and service to God, will see the snake slither away. He will be able to continue his service uninterrupted. One who receives an abundance of worldly pleasures and continues his service of God, will continue to receive them. He will be able to continue his service, while the pleasures will not interrupt him. The true servant of God is not interrupted either by pain or abundance.

Man as a Hired Watchman

God gave man desires and yearning, to use appropriately; then He gave him the body, a vessel that can contain holiness, and asked that all of His gifts be watched carefully. Just as one who is hired to watch an object is responsible if it is damaged by accident, so too man's soul. He will be asked if something is amiss with it. How then can he be declared innocent? Only by having the owner with him. By totally ignoring his needs in favor of devotion to God, the Master will be present with him; and when the master is present, he is inculpable for any wrongdoing.

Logically, we can make man responsible for every instance of weakness and failure. After all, he did it, and if it failed it was his fault. The truth is, though, that some things are beyond man's reach. If he cannot accomplish it, then he just couldn't. He therefore should not be discouraged, and should continue striving for higher goals.

Taking Credit

God is He who gives us life, health, and energy to observe His commandments. Hence we cannot take credit for the good deeds that we do. We could never have done them without the help of God! On the other hand, to subject our desire to God's desire, that only we can do. We have the choice and free will, and it is thus our doing. For that we can take credit.

And God, too, rewards us for overpowering our lust. We gave up "our world" for His; He therefore gives us "His world" in ours.

Free Will

Man has free will and can choose his life's path every moment. We might assume that only the righteous enjoy this free will, while the wicked have no use for it, but it is just the opposite! The righteous have already chosen a life of faith and Torah. They would rather have no choice: no struggles, no tests, only continual spiritual growth. On the other hand, the wicked always want choice, to have the volition and power to do more wickedness.

The Gift of Will

One of the greatest divine gifts to mankind is free will. It is the way God created man's mind, allowing him to do God's will or not to do it. It is his choosing completely.

Now man could think, "God could have controlled my will. After all, He is the absolute ruler. And now that He has given me a choice, how could I use that power against Him?" Those are certainly lofty and beautiful thoughts. Yet the physical longings, lusts, and yearnings of the world overpower such thoughts. How then can man ever be saved from continuing to pursue purely physical needs? First, man must trust God as a teacher and guide, and refuse to do evil—for any reason. By refusing, and not indulging and defiling himself with evil, he will realize the beauty of choosing it; he will come to understand it with thought and logic.

One Good Deed, and then Another

If a man has erred and strayed off the path, it is impossible for him to set himself right in one move: because as far as he has traveled away, he must travel just as far to get back. There are fools who, discovering the error of their ways, decide to right themselves in one move. Days later, realizing that they are still far from the mark, they surrender to despair and refuse to try again. However, by starting with merely one good deed, a man can build his confidence to do good. We must seize that good deed to prove to ourselves our spiritual capabilities. If we can do one good deed, we can do another, and another. Thus we move out of despondency to self-confidence.

The Princess

The soul of man is the princess from the palace of the King. It floods us with light and energy, and is the channel for infinite holiness and eternal bliss. Yet man unabashedly takes the princess and goes to the most vile and corrupt places, dragging her through the mud. How can we ever hope to return to the King's palace with the princess? How will we bear our shame?

Through repentance, not only is man's heart transformed, but all his actions are changed to good deeds. Because we, too, are children from the King's palace, we therefore mustn't be ashamed to come back to the company of the princess. When we do, we will realize that she was never sullied at all: it was all an illusion.

The One Thing

Although God gave man free will to do what he wants, He asks of him one and only one thing: never to forget that God is the giver of life. "Can you remember that although you have free will, I give you life?" asks God. On the other hand, man can say, "Well, You gave me free will, so it is not Your concern, really, if I remember You or not!" And God answers, "If you forget Me, then why did I create you? Why are you My creature?"

One who is righteous never forgets his Creator. If circumstances confront him, and it is humanly impossible to fight temptation, still he will be victorious. It would not be by choice, however, but because the *tzaddik*, the "righteous person," holds the thought of the Creator dearly in his mind, that God yanks him from the jaws of evil and to safety. He takes away his free will, so to speak, for that moment, and envelops it in divine thoughts. He makes him immune to evil, and thus the *tzaddik* remains unscathed by the challenge.

13

Unity

The Way of Peace

The world is made of billions of creatures, each different from the other. This affords at least two distinct paths for all of them: they can either get stuck on their diversity and foster isolation from each other, or they can find things in common and reach out to unite with them. The first is the way of adversity and warfare; the second is the way of co-operation and peace.

The creatures cannot find a common thread among themselves on their own. It is man who was ordained by God for this task. He has the ability to see below the surface—the surface which exhibits the differences between all things. He is able to bring unity and peace to the creation. When man falls short in his task, dire consequences can result. Competition and fighting erupt among plants and animals, with the annihilation of entire populations. Quibbling and wars erupt among nations, with massive destruction.

With the help of the Torah, man is able to heal the wounds of differences and bring peace to the whole world. Unfortunately, because of his shortcomings, this will not happen before the *Moshiach* comes, when the lamb and the lion, the sheep and wolf, the boy and the viper will live together in peace and harmony.

Union

The world of nature has an inner spiritual core. All of it together is contained in the Torah, which is the literary embodiment of the world of the spirit. Still, every created thing has its own spiritual kernel. How does the inner core of nature unite with the Torah? It becomes one when we observe the mitzvos, the commandments of God. By using our physical body and physical objects in the service of God, we respond to their inner spiritual core. The command of God to do His will and the command in the inner core of nature unite and become one.

One Divine Command

The world was created with ten divine commands, and it is our task to live with a sensitivity to those commands. All the commands, however, are but the one singular desire of God that there be a world. So really all the ten commands are but one single command. Those who are in tune to the ten commands, who see in each created thing the word of God, are able to someday reach the level of experiencing the one command. Their entire life, every living moment, is focused on

the will of God; their life also becomes united and insepa-
rable, and they experience fulfillment every moment.

Spiritually Connected

In the spiritual realm everything is connected. Although it
appears as if the *tzaddikim*, the "righteous," have nothing
to do with the *rasha'im*, the "wicked," with whom they live,
they are connected with them spiritually. The righteous who
are among the evildoers are like roses among the thorns. It
is their deeds that bring merit and spiritual energy to their
surroundings: it is because of them that the evildoers are
able to exist. That spiritual energy creates waves, and sparks
enter the hearts of the *rasha'im* that ignite opportunities of
repentance.

Even if we lead a sheltered life, with humility and fear of
God, Torah study and observing the commandments, we
are far from being isolated. We are connected, and one way
or another must do something for those around us, by deed,
by word, or by prayer.

One

There is a difference between "the first" and "one." First is
the beginning of the number series, but one is a unity, a
being who is unified with the roots of oneness. Therefore,
while first is within nature itself—anything can be the
first—one is higher than the natural world.

Similarly, some nations are the first in one thing or another, but the Jewish people are one. They are united in the
Oneness of God, and are therefore in a realm higher than
the world of nature.

Forget or Remember

A human being is flesh and blood, with passions, errors, and mistaken paths. How will he ever complete the mission that God has sent him to do? He forgot his mission and is distracted by thousands of things surrounding him. The only way he can ever accomplish his mission is by ignoring, forgetting completely, the vanities of this world. Then the memory of his heavenly commission—when he was made to swear that he will be righteous, not wicked—will return. He will remember without erring. Although thousands of attractions beckon, they will seem to him merely as an illusion, because the entire physical existence is but a corridor to enter the World to Come. Who but a fool would linger in the vestibule of a palace, when the king is waiting inside to bestow every imaginable pleasure?

Thus, those who forget, will remember, and those who remember, will forget.

The Center of Everything

In studying nature, we notice that from the tiniest creation, the atom, to the largest galaxies, there are central loci, points around which everything revolves. Metaphorically, they all point to the Creator, the central point of all that exists. In man also there is a central point, his soul, around which his life should revolve. Similarly, in the human race there are the Jewish people, who guard the revelation of the oneness of God and of the purpose in the creation. They were set aside as the children of Abraham, who chose and perfected himself in the task of revealing God's kingdom. Therefore, while it is out of the ordinary for a human being to have visions and revelations of the future, it is totally natural for the Jewish people. Representing God on earth, they too are the past, present, and future. Their visions and prophesies, their teachings and writings have fueled centuries of yearning for a better future and a more humane image of man.

Unity

In a unified whole there is interaction and cooperation. This is true among people: a society whose members work with interdependence, helping to fulfill each other's needs, has true unity. They are one. Similarly, in an animal, its parts help one another achieve its goal of survival and reproduction. Even in the microscopic realm, the cooperation within the organism unites all its parts. Wherever we look, from the awesomely large to the infinitesimally small, unity grows from the connectedness of the parts to the whole. Man too, is whole when all of him, every part of him, is receiving life from his spiritual essence.

The spiritual realm is the same. All of God's commandments are dependent one on the other. All of them together compose the word of God: God's love for the world and His teaching which brings unity to them. By connecting our deeds to the Torah, we unify our body with the one singular vitality. Because they are all nurtured from the same source, they mesh and become one.

In Harmony

In heaven God's light is revealed and bare, while on earth it is hidden. Each of us, also, is made of heaven, our soul, and earth, our body. While our soul sees the light of God clearly, His light is obscured to the body. One who is in harmony and unites his body and soul, will find the light of God on earth as well.

The Soul and the Body

Man's soul is from the spiritual world, and is as an alien on the material earth. His body, on the other hand, is from the physical world and is an alien to the spiritual world. After a lifetime, the body withers and dies and the soul lives eternally. This apparent dichotomy is resolved with the Torah, God's teachings. He gave us 613 commandments: 248 positive commandments to humble the 248 limbs, and 365 negative commandments to humble the 365 sinews. While the physical nature of man is humbled, his soul is uplifted and strengthened.

With each act done by man, the question is: who will be the stranger, the body or the soul? When man turns away from the physicality of the world and focuses on the spiritual within everything, then the light of his soul lights his life.

The Spiritual Body

The toes are connected to the foot, and the foot to the leg, the leg to the thigh, then to the hip, the midriff, torso, neck, and head. Similarly, the 613 commandments of the Torah are each the spiritual energy for one of the 613 parts of the body. By observing all of them, the spiritual body of man connects bit by bit, is built, and becomes one. All of it is then energized by the unified spirit of God, and a divine intelligence flows through it all.

Brain, Heart, and Liver

The kingdom on earth is like the kingdom of heaven. The word *melech*, mem-lamed-chof, means "king," and each letter is significant: mem signifies *mo-ach*, "the brain," intellect and the soul; lamed signifies *lev*, "the heart," emotions and spirit; and chof signifies *ko-ved*, "the liver," blood and the life of man. The soul of man is continually in God's presence. The spirit rises and descends between the spiritual and the material spheres, and the life of man is in the liver. Man is the king over them all and it is in his hands to bring unity to all of them.

To Desire One

By unifying all his desires to serve God, a man can cleave to God's unique oneness. His desires are unified with God's desire, and he is ready to do whatever God may tell him: he is then redeemed from all his exiles. Similarly, when the Jewish people unify and have one singular desire to serve God, they are a vessel for His command and desire: they are then instantaneously redeemed from their exile and are forever free.

In Their Footsteps

Jewish children always follow in the footsteps of their forefathers. Had they continued to collect and unify, the final redemption would surely come.

Two Strengths

The Jewish people have two abilities: the first is to separate themselves from the pursuit of merely materialistic pleasure, and the second is to devote and connect themselves to divine holiness.

Unified

The divine sparks of light are in all things, even in the most remote and wicked. They are the unifying force of the creation. Then there is the spark itself, its light, which is the essence of them all: that is the Torah, the word of God.

Our forefathers worked within the world of nature to bring about spiritual unity. And Moses went straight to the Tree of Life, the Torah, the essence of the light. Not everyone can do that, however, and many must struggle to reach the inner world of the spirit through the Torah.

The Tiniest Start

Even if the Jewish people are lowered to the earth, with the least good deeds, by uniting as one they receive great blessings. Suddenly they stir and yearn for God's service. Although it is but the meagerest beginning, God blesses it and values it greatly. With that small step in the right direction, they can continue on to the highest level.

The Holy Tongue

The ability of speech is connected to the soul. Because the soul is spiritual and holy, speech is basically the holy tongue, *loshon hakodesh*. Although animals also communicate with grunts, barks, whistles, and whinnies, those are inferior to speech. Speech is a very advanced form of verbal communication.

What possible holiness can be communicated by speech? Declaring the kingdom of God. That is true *loshon hakodesh*, and its task was given to the Jewish people. To the degree that the nations of the world get close to such declarations, they too partake in the holy tongue; but when they use their language to declare plurality of masters, war, and enslavement to natural forces, their speech is no better than the braying of donkeys.

Let us lift up our speech to the level of the holy tongue, and use it in the service of God and mankind.

No Attachments

God desired to make the world, and that desire is still present in every item of creation. It is hidden, however, inside the physical part of the universe. When man desires that physical crust, he becomes attached to it, and it separates him from the divine. The way to reach the inner core is by throwing aside all attachments.

When we yearn to recognize the desire of God, to know and do His will, we must rid our heart of attachments to the world. When we do, the inner desire for God in each thing will be revealed. The path to follow becomes clear, and we move straight ahead toward our goal.

The One and Only

God is the ultimate of oneness and singularity. There is not another like Him in or out of the universe. He is the one and only Creator and God. Created things, on the other hand, are in the realm of numbers and are more than one. Even the heavenly angels, try as they may to be as united as possible, are not one and only. Their unity is only possible by connecting to their roots, their Creator. And that is only possible if at first they unite among themselves.

How is the creation able to unite? It is because everything was created with the twenty-two letters of the Hebrew alphabet and its combinations. These twenty-two letters are different sounds of the one and only God's name. So that the twenty-two letters are really all one. When physical creatures who are naturally separated try to unite, they are uniting their letters into the one name of God. They connect with the oneness of God and therefore they also become one.

This teaches that those who cause quarrels and disunity destroy the spiritual nature of the world and will not succeed. Those who strive for peace and unity are imitating the work of God and will prevail.

14

Faith

Higher than the Angels

An angel is aware that the sole purpose of its existence is its divine mission: without that, it would not exist. There is never any other type of awareness for an angel. Not so the human being: he too is only on earth to accomplish God's mission, but he can blunder and think that he is alive for purely physical pursuits. How then will he be a witness for God's kingdom? He must surrender his desires, and humble himself and his very life to the mission that God wants of him. Because man has to work so hard to be a witness for God's kingdom, that witnessing is on a much higher level than even that of the angels.

Firm in Faith

The righteous do not get impressed nor intimidated by the outward circumstances of their lives. They remain steadfast, and stay firm and consistent in their faith. They do not change with each changing moment, but allow the moments and changes to bounce off them.

A Jew Is Thankful

The reason the Jewish people are called *Yehudim* is from the word *ho-da-ah*, "thankfulness." We are constantly thanking God for every big or small favor or gift we receive from Him. Since we do, we also always look for the good, the redemption, the light within the darkness. We are the ones who for thousands of years have taught, in the deserts of the Middle East, the true faith and belief in positive outcomes. Through the well-traveled trade routes of spices, precious stones, and fabrics, the faith of our fathers spread far and wide the world over. When we have difficulty, we ought to talk it out with ourselves, how the difficulty may turn out as a spiritual benefit to us. This is the tradition of the Jewish people, who in their greatest difficulty do not forget God as the source of all events.

Entrance through the Tiny Gate

The presence of God is everywhere, and there is no place where he is not found. But the gate to get to it is the tiny dot, the holy spark, the soul of man. Entering that tiny dot, we are suddenly in the presence of that which fills the entire universe. This is quite unimaginable in our dimension, but it is so. To enter it we must subject our being to the dot of holiness.

Remembering the One

In the highest spiritual spheres there is unity, and with each descending level there is more and more plurality. As a symbol of this the Jewish people were the least populous of the nations. Those who do not forget the One even when they are among the seventy wolves, will soon merit redemption.

The Two Hearts

The heart of man has two aspects: the heart of the learned and the heart of the fool, the enlightened and the ignorant; with constant conflict between the two. When one is strong the other is weakened, and is in exile. Man must work hard to enlighten both parts of his heart.

The light of the soul, on the other hand, is unified and is a steady glowing light. When that light shines its rays into man's heart, all conflict ceases and the heart becomes one and enlightened. It is redeemed.

Prayer from the conflicted heart is with pain and anguish. But the prayers of the enlightened mind are a yearning to be with God.

The Eyes and the Heart

The heart and the mind belong to God. We are not at liberty to look for, nor to rationalize out of, His realm. Similarly, when God does not want you to see or feel something, you won't. If He does want you to feel and see, you will—even if you don't like it.

Spiritual "Time"

When a Gentile loves the lifestyle of the Jewish people and converts to Judaism, he takes all his days and raises them to a higher spiritual level. That is similar to the work of the entire creation. In the physical world, time is made of moments, hours, days, weeks, months, and years. Our work is to lift up the four-dimensional time of this plane to another dimension, spiritual "days" which exist in the spiritual universe. When we do, all our days are full of life and vitality.

There will come a day when all our days will be repaired, and suddenly the days will not end: they will be endless and eternal.

Faith and Perseverance

It is only with faith that a man exerts energy and works to uncover the hidden light. Otherwise, why would he bother? Perhaps there is nothing there. By believing and persevering, he reaches enlightenment. Thus, true enlightenment is the result of faith and perseverance.

The First Words

A mother waits with joyful anticipation for her child to say his first word. That first word will be his real and true expression. Wouldn't the mother be shocked, though, if while she were waiting his first word, he would suddenly turn and say, "Mommy, I hate you!"

Similarly, each human being has something to say, and so do the Jewish people. They are here to declare God's kingdom, but cannot, in the exile. While they cannot declare and say their word, they must refrain from saying anything contradictory. That would really be sad and unfit. Here they can't even express their own word, and yet they say other things? It is better they remain silent till they can give full expression to their true words.

Both in Pain and Joy

The Jewish people accept their travails with love for God. They do so for the sake of He who has challenged them with great distress and trouble. Still, that is far easier than it is to remember God in times of joy. To think of how joyful one is to be receiving God's gifts is harder than accepting pain. He who rejoices for God's sake will enjoy the strength of God's presence when he is in distress.

Faith in the Darkness

There are times when the divine providence is revealed. It is clear, and we "know." Such is possible on the Sabbath. But during the weekdays, the days of work, when we think that we are accomplishing things, we need faith. The kingdom of God is hidden, it is covered and in darkness. But those who persevere and remain with their faith will see a great light in the end.

Resignation

A creature can either be in a state of rest or in a state of agitation. It finds its rest when it is in total submission to the Creator. Then there is no pain from wanting, because whatever happens he accepts with total resignation. How could he possibly want something else? The Creator is He who has granted it to him.

Ultimately, when are we in pain? When we are not satisfied with our lot; when we want our life to be different than it is now. But when we are in awe of God, and realize that everything is from Him, then we have no anxiety or turmoil in our heart. We are content.

15

A Servant's Wisdom

Enjoy the Gift

One who sells an item is only interested in the monetary profit it brings; but one who gives a gift is interested that the recipient enjoys it, too. Therefore, if he gives a well, he also gives him the path to get to the well. Similarly, when God gives a gift, he gives the capacity to enjoy the gift, too.

Being Quiet

There are two types of quiet. One is when man cannot even call out; the pain is so great that he cannot get a voice out of his mouth. The other is when he realizes that although he is capable of calling out, it is better to remain silent.

New Path

Just as God creates a new path for the world as He renews
it, so the true servant of God creates a new path for his service to God. If we are not fortunate enough to create a new
path, then at least let us renew our stirring and enthusiasm
to serve God with love.

What's New?

There is nothing new under the sun; in the natural world
there is no renewal. However, if one totally subjects his self,
and sacrifices his being for the service of God, he experiences renewal. Normally, a human being does not throw
aside his basic instincts: it is the rule of nature. But one who
has given up the rules of the world is above and beyond the
natural world, and there renewal is found.

Hurdles

With each upward step in spiritual development, we can
expect a hurdle to be in our way. It is not put there to upset
our accomplishment; it is there to make each step of the
way harder for us. With each struggling move we make, we
gain our spiritual level permanently.

Royal Power

A servant who asks permission from the king to do his bidding acts with the power of royalty. Whatever he does has

the name of royalty attached to it. The angels do the same when they call to each other and ask permission to praise God's name. Similarly, the Jewish people, whose name *Yisroel* is synonymous with "Servants of God," are the royal representatives who uncover God's kingdom. The more loyal they are to their task, the more their name is appropriate for them. Finally, when they complete their mission, their name becomes complete and clings to them as skin on the body. It is theirs and they fit into it perfectly.

Rising Above

There are those who rise above their difficulties, and others who overpower their difficulties and vanquish them. God lifts up the lowly and lowers the haughty. He gives strength to the Jewish people who are lowly to withstand the abuse, persecution, and oppression of their surroundings. That is one of the greatest miracles.

Being with God

One who lowers himself despite the fact that he knows God is with him will continue to have God with him, even if he is lowered to the ground. That spiritual level, to be even-tempered regardless of the circumstances, is a difficult one to reach. Regardless if one is high or low, one feels equally cared for by God.

Similarly there are the busy and anxious days of the week, and the serene quiet day of Sabbath rest. He who quiets himself from all anxiety in order to enjoy a quiet Sabbath, God too will bring quiet when he is anxious.

Breaching the Wall

We are creatures of the Creator. We are very far removed
from His holiness and spirituality; it is as if there were an
impregnable wall between us and God. How then can this
wall be broken through? By God's love. God loves the Jewish people as a father loves his children. To the degree that
they love Him as their Father, He treats them as His children. Then no wall is strong enough to separate God from
His people.

Searching for Treasure

Two people could be looking for something. One looks for a
lost object, while the other searches for buried treasures. The
former is pained and frantic when looking, saddened by loss;
when he finds his object, he is not overjoyed, because he already had it before. But he who searches for hidden treasures
is not anxious, and is overjoyed when he finds them.

When we search for the spiritual, we must combine the
two. We must possess the urgency of searching for something
lost, and then have the great joy of finding buried treasure.

That is really the truth. Whatever spirit we find was really
there, but buried deep within our heart. Thus we can search
for it with urgency: we did once have it, but we must be
thrilled with surprise when we uncover its location and nature.

To Work in the World

The work of God's servant on earth is not done by isolating
himself. Rather, it is done by reaching out to the world at
large and connecting it to God's holiness.

Breaking Habits

There are times when we get stuck in our habits and there seems no way out. Then God puts us into exile, and redeems us: thus our old habits are broken and a new way is found.

Light of the World

Each human being is the lamp of God, and He lights it with a soul, a spark of divine holiness. The Jewish people are the lamp that contains all the individual members of the tribe of Israel, and the nations are the lamp that contains the Jewish people. Thus, when the Jewish people subject their being and open their hearts to God, and are vessels only to Him, they are then the light of the world.

The Complete Return

God is the source of all unity. Although the physical world is made of parts and is in disunity, man was sent to unite it. But it causes him great pain when he realizes that he could have stayed in the unity of heaven rather than suffer the disunity of the earth. It awakens a great longing in him to return to God; in the deepest sense, it is the root of repentance.

If man returns to God with his whole heart and soul, he can fix all that is broken, and unite all that has been rent asunder.

Man and the Angels

The word of God, its spiritual essence, is in every creation in the form of an angel. Likewise, our relationship with the creation is prescribed by the commandments, the mitzvos, of the Torah. The mitzvah teaches us how to deal with the world. It instructs us how to relate to the spiritual essence, the angel within. Thus, although the angels seem to be spiritually higher than humans, they are not. It is the humans who awaken the angels' energy by doing the mitzvah. On the other hand, who gives man the energy to do a mitzvah? The angels. So there is a circle of energy, from the angel to man and from man to the angel.

Kindness and Mercy

There is kindness and mercy. It is kindness to give a gift to one who is in need. But mercy comes from assessment, contemplation, and mind. It grows out of the relationship of the giver to the recipient. It is from the truth of one being to the truth of the other being.

God gives the gift of life and sustenance to every creature regardless of its actions, good or evil, but to those who are close to Him in truth, He relates with mercy. While kindness is beneficial, mercy is deeper and infinite.

The Hands and the Head

The hands are like a handle, a means of reaching the spiritual. But the hands are also implements, tools with which man can harm, destroy, or annihilate. Therefore the hands need strong guidance, to be harnessed as a horse, to go in the right direction. This is accomplished with the tefilin, phylacteries, which we tie on the hand. We tie them, binding the hands: harness, guide them.

When man focuses his actions, his intellect is free to fathom the greatness of the Almighty. Therefore the tefilin are merely placed on the head. They don't need the harnessing and tying, after the hands are tied to the right place.

Attraction and Repulsion

Two emotions are opposites: one attracts, the other repels. One is love, the other is fear. In our relationship with God they strengthen each other. Love of God leads to awe of Him, and fear of Him leads to love of Him. They intertwine and fuse together, and become one.

No "Patch-up Jobs"

When we move to a higher spiritual level, we ought to be sure and firm. We should not have to go back down, to fix our weak spots and return again. That would be a "patch-up job."

With Our Effort

Man has the opportunity to cleanse himself of the barriers which block his path to God. In the measure of his hard work and effort to remove all obstacles, God too, allows him to receive the Holy Spirit.

Spirit when Deserved

There are two paths for divine inspiration: one is a gift from God, the other is a reward for hard work. A divine gift in the hands of a material being is foreign and has no place to stay. If on the other hand it is received because of hard work, as a reward, it rightfully belongs to the recipient. It has a place, and is bound with strong connections to the person.

Deeds and Awe

The awe and fear of God, as essential as it is, is incomplete without deeds. The deed, fathered by awe, is a reflection of man's heart.

A Minor Commandment

One of God's commands may seem insignificant compared to some other goal. It may even be logical to ignore the smaller command in favor of bigger outcomes. Yet that is not God's desire. We need to observe God's command now, regardless of our reasons.

Step by Step

Even if we are not ready to risk everything to observe God's commandments, we would certainly observe them if conditions were more favorable. There is some part of us, even if minuscule, which wants to do the will of God. Therefore, little by little, we can rise, step by step, to the level of our forefathers. They have already paved the way and planted the seeds of total resignation to God's will in the hearts of their offspring. As distant as we feel from their spiritual level, we can get there, if we are stubborn enough to persist.

Being Part of the Collective

One needs to concern himself only that the honor of God's kingdom be exalted. It should not matter who accomplishes it, whether it is he or someone else. He should be happy that someone, rather than no one, did it. This can only happen in the mind of one who totally subjects himself to the collective soul of the Jewish people. Then he is part of the team that reveals God's Kingdom. He is proud and happy for each member of the team who accomplishes the team goal.

On the other hand, he who separates himself from the rest of the Jewish people, and thinks that he is on a solitary campaign, will be jealous and even try to thwart others who do the job better than he. Therefore our sages have taught, "He who minimizes his own honor, and maximizes God's honor, will accomplish his goal."

God Is Looking at the World

When God created the world, He looked at it, and saw that it was good. That was a divine look, far different than a human one. We look and merely see. God's "look" is His loving care, which sustains the world to this very day. It is awesome to realize that when we look at something, God is looking at it, too. Those who believe and understand this are privileged to see the world in an entirely new way.

If You Are Far, Come Near

All life is a gift from God, and He alone is the One who puts it into every living being. There are those in whom the divine gift is apparent, and others in whom their body conceals it. We might err to think that a man in whom the spirit is more apparent has more reason to draw himself closer to God, but the opposite is true. He who is weaker, who is further removed from spirit, should struggle and strive to come near to God.

Love of God

There are two types of love for God. One is *ahavas olam*, "everlasting love," the love for God the creator: it is the result of contemplating the universe. The other is *ahava rabah*, "great love," the love which is beyond the physical, and is infinite.

The universe, as vast as it seems, is still finite compared to that which is beyond it. And therefore the love that is based on it is finite and small, compared to the infinite. Similarly, man is a microcosm, a model of the creation. He who is on the lower levels will feel his body controlling him; but he who is on a higher level, his love for God being even bigger than the world, will be in control of his body.

Sins That Are Not Sins

Sin depends upon the awareness of the individual. When one is of tender age, he is not culpable for the sins he commits. Not even the most righteous are free of sin. What is sin for a person on a very high spiritual level, however, is not considered sin for one on a low level; and the levels are endless, as is the heart of man. Thus there are sins that are not considered sins, and there are actions that are considered sin only for angels, who are high above sinfulness.

The Soul and the Body

The soul of man is spiritually so lofty that his physical being can hardly understand it, just as the human brain, although part of the human body, seems not to belong because of its abstract functions, yet is just as much a part of the human body as the heart and the liver. Similarly, the soul is integrally bound with the body, yet hardly understood. This concept can restore man's faith in God and improve his relationship with mankind, as it becomes clear to him that God, too, is removed from the physical realm, yet we can cleave to Him and His ways.

Wake to a New Day

Each day that dawns is different than the one that preceded it. Each has its particular freshness and newness, starting at dawn and ending at nightfall. The day ends so that a new day can start: thus is the creation renewed, and the creatures need not wallow in an old dilapidated world. The world of yesterday is gone, a new one begins with fresh opportunity and providence.

One needs to be open to the newness of each day and week, each month and year.

He Helps Us Do Good Deeds

We can do deeds of merit and hope that God will reward us for them, but we have to realize that those deeds came to us through the kindness of God. He gave us the health, strength, spirit, and understanding to do them. Therefore, no matter how purely benevolent, righteous, ethical, and loving we are, we constantly depend on the kindness of God.

No Attachments

We are messengers of God. All the good that we do is by the will and power of God. On the other hand, if we insist that the accomplishments are ours and become attached to them, we limit them and endanger their success. We must have no attachments to our good deeds, and constantly hope for the help of God. Then let God do what He wills, we have already done ours.

Each Day

There are 365 days in the year and 365 negative commandments, as if each day reminds us to keep another one of them. Each day is also an opportunity to understand God on a higher level. So it seems that the more days that pass, the higher we ought to be spiritually. The problem is that we don't accumulate the days. We don't take the level of yesterday along with us into today. We need to remember everything we learned yesterday, today, and each day. Then we will have a life filled with days.

We Are Sons and Servants

Each of us possesses a physical body and a spiritual essence, each of which relates in a different way to God. The spiritual spark, which is heavenly and divine, relates as a son to his father. The physical body, on the other hand, relates as a servant to his master. A son does anything for his father because he loves him, while the servant must humble himself totally to his master. Although we would prefer to think of ourselves as sons to our Father, we must also appreciate our servant-like aspect. After all, it is no small privilege to be a servant of the King of Kings, the Creator.

Similarly, each created thing also has the two aspects of son and servant. The spiritual spark in each creation is the offspring, and the outer shell, the physical reality, is the servant.

Those who would like to be as sons to their Father, what can they do? They need to subject themselves to the spiritual essence in each thing and situation. Wherein lies the spirituality in this thing that is before them? By seeking it and finding it, they act as the sons of the Most High. They look for and find His honor and kingdom, just as sons who would protect the honor of their father's kingdom.

By being a devoted servant and working diligently for the Master, one can elevate himself and rise to the level of son.

Not to Miss a Day

There should not be a day or a moment without spiritual growth and uplifting. Each day is waiting for us to reach the spiritual level which will serve as the foundation for the next higher level. Once we are mature enough for this idea, we must not allow the days to slip by. If we do, we will be missing many levels of spirituality which we could already have attained.

Out of Prison

Not only can man remove himself from prison by believing in and serving the one and only God, but he can also remove each creation from its prison. All the prisons are the finite physical crust of the creation. But with faith in the spiritual, the infinite aspect of the creature is revealed and the prison of limitations falls away.

Fear to Live without Love for God

People think that the attributes of being accepting, loving, easygoing, tender, and caring are easily available. They also think that a relationship with God based on kindness and dependence is available for everyone. The truth is that those who always hope for God's kindness are God-fearing, and have therefore been granted the privilege; except the fear of Him is hidden within the love, but is revealed when put to the test.

There are those who want to live with tolerance, whose tolerance is then challenged. Those who fear to live with intolerance will not succumb, even in dire circumstances; but others, whose tolerance is only a lack of opinion, will fail the test and become intolerant.

Those who fear to live without the love of God will not give it up when put to the test.

Time Is within the Created World

Creation includes all of physical reality, and also time. God desired that events should flow from the past to the present, and from the present to the future. Each creature lives within that time system and cannot jump backwards or forwards. This is not true for the spirit which God placed into man: its realm is above and beyond the created world, and therefore beyond time.

Those who use their spirit to pursue physical pleasure for its own sake, become slaves to time. Lacking spiritual content, they have no wisdom. On the other hand, those who use the physical world to achieve spiritual goals, are beyond time. Their deeds affect the present, the future, and even the past. Since their spirit dominates, they are filled with wisdom.

Fresh and New

After reevaluating personal events we realize God's providence in a deeper way, and experience His imminence. That is our wisdom and understanding. One needs to guard and save those revelations, so that he can draw inspiration from them; they need to be kept fresh, just as we first experienced them, as stirring as a newfound treasure. Otherwise they become old, worn out, and useless. As part of our nature, although helping us to grow, they no longer have the power to inspire.

Wisdom is the knowledge of our inner essence, the spirit within us. Each time we are inspired with God's presence we need to connect it to the spirit within. Our spirit, which is a holy spark from the highest realms, is always fresh and new, here and now, remembered and not forgotten.

Always with Kindness

Even when God judges and is ready to mete out judgment, he first clothes it in mercy and kindness. No matter what, kindness is never forgotten, and is on the right, the side without forgetfulness.

The Loftiest Motivation

One's heart should be fired up to do a good deed in the utmost and perfect way. Then even if he is unable to complete it as planned, at least he was motivated by the most noble intentions. The energy for his deed, then, came from the highest of places, and God in His great mercy will consider his deed as if he did complete it in every detail.

Love and Awe

One can serve God with a love so deep that every fiber of his body is stirred by it, every breath filled with it; he is drawn to the word of God and its inspiration; he is motivated to action and is sensitive to every command; he is strong beyond strength to climb mountains, wade streams, and go through fire for the One he loves.

There are times, however, that the awe and fear of God go even beyond love. Even when love is inactive and the attraction wanes, the awe of the creature before his Creator in fear and trembling makes one do His will.

Thus we need both love and fear of God to complete our service to Him.

God Provides Our Needs

Each creature has needs, and is busy with them most of the time. It needs food, shelter, rest, to procreate, and so on. It actively pursues its needs with energy and cunning, getting attached to the pursuit and the accomplishment. In man this attachment creates a barrier between him and the Creator.

Saying, "I have a need and I am filling it," leaves the Creator out, and the creature becomes attached to his own powers.

When man removes the barriers from his heart, God likewise removes the spiritual barriers between him and the Creator. He thus stands face to face with God.

Giving It All Away

One is more attached to the spiritual level achieved through one's hard work than that which God grants as an outright gift. This has a positive and a negative consequence. On the one hand, man works much harder for things that he deems his own; on the other, he is less likely to appreciate the divine influence enabling him to attain it. Therefore it is even better if man resigns his ownership of all spiritual achievement. Thus he is able to ascend in holiness and attain his spiritual goals.

Without Distractions

The servant of God is focused on his life's work. He is not distracted, saying, "Now, where was I?" He knows constantly where he is and where he is heading. It is all one and the same activity: he is not involved in fragmentary activities, but is in one continual movement toward God. When he goes to sleep and awakens, he needn't ask, "Now, where was I?" He knows that he is in the very place that he was before he went to sleep. Just as prior to sleeping he yearned to serve God, the instant he awakens, his thoughts are of God and of his yearning to serve Him.

A Miraculous People

There is an observable regularity in nature. It is ruled by
laws which do not change, allowing us to predict events.
But there are also unpredictable events, and events that
do not conform to laws. That is how the Jewish people
exist: they are not subject to the laws and regularity of
the natural world. They live by a different order, the order
of miracles. Therefore, although according to nature the
Jewish people should have long disappeared and their land
have been reduced to sand, they persist. They have survived countless attempts at annihilation and destruction.
They flourish still, and their culture pervades much of the
Western world, influencing its ideas and institutions.

The Smallest Command

God promised Abraham that his descendants would be a
great nation: they would be witnesses for God's kingdom,
and they would do God's will and good deeds to the end of
time. Yet as soon as God commanded him to sacrifice his
son Isaac—which would have brought all those promises
to an end—he went immediately, although God's command
seemed like a mistake that would wipe out a potential nation and millions of good deeds, beyond Abraham himself!
Yet he did not hesitate.

The lesson for us is that the smallest command of God
must be followed with the same enthusiasm as the one we
think is the more important. We cannot use our logic to
decide which of them to do. When He commands we must
obey.

On the Path of Our Forefathers

Our forefathers Abraham, Isaac, and Jacob were totally devoted and dedicated to revealing God's kingdom. They prepared a path for all their descendants. Although we may not have the same resolve and dedication, although we may not be ready to ignore our needs for God's sake, still we have the path. The path is already there, and all we need do is take the first step, even if it be a halting, weak, and unsure one; once we do take the step, we are on the path of our forefathers and can eventually reach the goal.

The Tests and the Miracles

The words "miracle" and "test" both have an identical Hebrew root: *neis*. It is because of the tests in which our forefathers proved their absolute devotion to the will of God, towering above human nature, that God relates to their descendants with miracles beyond the laws of nature. Besides, the Jewish people would never survive without miracles in the face of the opposition of the seventy nations and their angels. They need miracles for their very life, as they need to live with absolute resolve and superhuman devotion to their principles.

Those Who Are Far Are Drawn Near

There are times when we are discouraged and depressed about our meager accomplishments. We feel unworthy to be near God and His holiness.

The truth is, though, that our imperfection is all the more reason why we will succeed in getting close to God and staying in His presence, because God draws near even those who are far. When He draws the near ones nearer, not nearly as much energy is required as when He draws near those who are far: therefore the imperfect ones are drawn with more force, and come closer even than the righteous.

Limits of Love

Love and kindness are the highest of virtues, and are without limits in the spiritual world; but in this physical world they must have vessels to contain and protect them. Without protection one can love even evil itself. The virtue of judgment guides us as to whom and when to love.

God Is Our Witness

The Jewish people are the witnesses to God and His kingdom. They declare the presence of God despite the fact that He is unseen in this false world of illusion. However in the celestial spheres, the world of truth, where the angels are, all this is unnecessary. Similarly, God is witness for the Jewish people in the heavenly spheres. He loves their service even more than that of the angels. But on earth He needn't be witness for them, for who but the Jewish people are witnesses to His kingdom? Who thanks Him a hundred times a day, and is ready to give up all for His honor? Only the Jewish people.

Credit and Creation

The purpose of all that God created was in order that His honor be increased. This honor is made manifest through the work of the *tzaddikim*, "the righteous," who constantly bring honor to His name. Therefore the entire creation is to their credit, and they are rewarded for it.

The Light Shines Through

The spiritual goal of the creation is to lift the physical to the level of the spiritual. For this purpose God had placed three levels of spiritual essence into our body: "the spirit," *nefesh*; "breath," *ru-ach*; and "soul," *neshama*. With these three we can raise the level of our three parts: the deed, the speech, and the thought. Each one of them can be elevated from the pursuit of purely physical goals to the pursuit of spiritual goals. This is why the fear of God is called *yiroh*, also meaning "to see." When we are in awe and fear of God, when we tremble to do His will in every facet of our life, we then see the truth. The light of our spiritual essence shines forth through our opaque physical nature, and we understand our spiritual purpose.

When we purify our body, becoming transparent to the light of God, the spirit echoes, and its light shines through. When the inside light touches the outside light, and the outside light touches the inside light, we are enlightened beings. Our purpose is clear, and we see infinitely into our past and future. Unfortunately, most do not reach this level till the instant of their death. It is then that most mortals see with sheer clarity the meaning of their deeds in the past, and their effect on the infinite future. But why wait, when with hard work one can reach this level sooner in one's lifetime?

Vessels for the Spirit

There are three partners in the formation of a child: the father, the mother, and the Creator. The physical body is formed of the biological material of the father and mother. Then the Creator places the heavenly spirit in its vessel.

Similarly, the commandments of the Torah are spiritual lights; they need physical vessels to hold them. These are the actual actions, the deeds themselves. The righteous are constantly creating vessels for the spirit of God. By observing the commandments, they make vessels for the spirit to enter the physical world.

Light to the Nations

Just as the Torah brings light to all of man's actions, so too, the Jewish people bring light to all the nations of the world. In fact, it is their job to uplift the creation.

How do they raise the creation to higher spiritual levels? By the way they relate to the earth, the animals, and the people, they set an example for others. Their caring attitude about the earth's productivity, as in the mitzvah of *shmitah*; their high regard for animal life, as in the mitzvah of *tzar baalei chaim*, forbidding one to cause pain to any living being; their laws concerning legal matters between man and man: all of these are beacons for the behavior of mankind.

About the Author

Moshe A. Braun is director of Hope Educational Services, servicing communities with educational innovations. He also directs the Free Jewish University, a Torah outreach program for college-age youth. A Holocaust survivor who has written and lectured on the subject at college campuses, he is also one of the pioneers in popularized hasidic ideas and thought through lectures and published articles. Braun has written more than ten books, including *The Talking B'somim Box* (1990), *Leap of Faith* (1992), *The Magic Comb* (1993), and *The Jewish Holy Days* (1996). He currently resides in New York with his wife and children.